WOMEN'S VOICES

FROM THE

MOTHER LODE

Other books in the Women's Voices Series
By Susan G. Butruille

Women's Voices from the Oregon Trail
Women's Voices from the Western Frontier

WOMEN'S VOICES

FROM THE

MOTHER LODE

Tales from the California Gold Rush

by
Susan G. Butruille

Original illustrations by
Kathleen R. Petersen

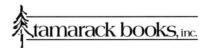
tamarack books, inc.

First edition, trade: September, 1998

10 9 8 7 6 5 4 3 2

Women's Voices™ Trademark pending.

ABOUT THE COVER: The cover was designed by Kathleen R.
Petersen, using the "Medallion Star with Flying Geese and
Shoo Fly Variation" quilt by Harriet Jane Pope Randolph,
1842–1848. Used by courtesy of Flora Jane Randolph Gorman
and the California Heritage Quilt Project. Photo of the Quilt is
by Sharon Risedorph. In addition, Ms. Petersen used the photo
of Manuella, courtesy of the Calaveras County Historical
Society, San Andreas, California. On the back cover, she used
a recent photo of Susan G. Butruille by R.E. Greffenius.

All photographs are by the author unless otherwise noted.

AUTHOR AND PUBLISHER NOTE: We take no responsibility for any
food prepared according to the "receipts" included within this
book. They are intended for reading only.

PUBLISHED BY:
Tamarack Books, Inc.
PO Box 190313
Boise, ID 83719-0313

Printed in the United States of America.

DEDICATION

To Griff—my best bro.

With special thanks to:
   Jacqueline Brodnitz, Lucile Bogue, Ed Gwilym,
Hanne Gwilym, Saundra Timberlake, Eloise
Gregory, Inge Zumwalt, Joe Zumwalt, Frank
Butruille, Meleah Eunsil Butruille, Tony Butruille,
Norm Jacobs, Phyllis Jacobs, Helen Mason, Jack
Mason, Julie Larson, Ron Katon, Ruth Katon,
Cynthia Ristity, Deborah Olsen, Kathy Gaudry,
Kathleen Petersen, Gail Ward, Kelly Perry, Kathy
Jones.

Once more my deepest gratitude to my mother, Ruth
Hendricks Greffenius, whose expertise and support
make this book possible; and to John, who kept me
going.

TABLE OF CONTENTS

PRELUDE

Oh who will come go with me?
I am bound for the promised land.
—popular song sung during the
westward migrations

I know a land far to the West. It is a land where golden hills shimmer in the golden sun. Stones of shining gold lie about, just waiting to be gathered. Hidden within the burnished mountains lies a lake of gold.

This land of gold is a land of fantasy, where the real is unreal, where things are not as they seem. It is a land of extremes.

To reach this golden land you must leave all you have known and loved. Like the Greek wanderer Jason and his Argonauts, you must travel great dis-

tances, on land or sea. You will fight strange creatures, scale mountains, and cross endless deserts. You will reach undreamed-of heights and sink to unimagined depths. You will meet grotesque monsters of hunger and sickness and terror, and wonders of magnificence and courage and compassion. You will praise heaven and curse hell. Everything you have ever known and everything you have ever believed will be tested.

You will see passing before you wondrous beauty and putrid ugliness. The sounds will rattle your senses. The smells will sicken and enchant. You will be rich and you will be poor. You will never be the same.

Strangers will aid you on your journey. Tricksters will tempt you to follow errant paths. Scoundrels lurking in the shadows will try to rob you of your riches and your soul.

Come to California. The land of gold.

Gold! The magical metal that glows like the sun. Gold! Bringer of fame and fortune, power, health, and long life!

Come to California. *El Dorado.* The gilded land.

Awaiting you are treasures untold. Riches unimagined. Passions unleashed. You may find your treasure or you may die trying. When you reach this golden land—if you do—you will be a stranger in a strange land.

Come, if you dare. Come—on the most fantastic journey you will ever know. Come to the Mother Lode of California—land of hope and despair, carnival and glory.

It will be a journey of high drama and low comedy. So bring along your masks. You'll need them.

INTRODUCTION

**[F]or nature makes it clear
that gold has a laborious begetting,
a hard guarding,
the greatest covetousness,
and its use lies between
pleasure and pain.**
—Diodorus of Sicily, 1st Century BCE

This book is a journey—a journey of the mind and soul, to perhaps the most fantastic episode in the history of the world—the California Gold Rush of 1849. At no other time in history did so many people come from so many places to such a small piece of land—all for the same purpose. They didn't come to conquer the people who already were there, though they did. They did come to scoop up the gold and go home rich, though most of them didn't.

The history of the California Gold Rush is steeped in magic and whimsy and mythology. It was as though Fortune had taken her magic wheel and whirled it madly around, scattering people and events at random here on the Mother of all Lodes of gold.

Mother Lode had different meanings to the people who met here. Mother Lode as a magical land of gold to be extracted and consumed. Mother Lode as the source of life to be respected and sustained.

There really was a Mother Lode. The people who had lived here for thousands of years knew their Mother Lode well. Their Mother Lode was the earth—source of all they needed to live and love and survive. And it came from the Grandparents. Many ancient peoples' stories tell of the Grandmother thinking into being the possibility of earth, the sea and sky and all their beings.

As long as the people respected and cared for Mother Earth, she would yield her riches: in clear flowing water, and in trees that bore fruit and provided bark and wood for shelter; in acorns and roots that could be pounded and ground to make bread, the staff of life; in grasses and insects that fed animals that provided food and warm skins for winter.

Many who swarmed into the people's country believed there to be a Mother Lode of gold—one source of gleaming gold that would bring them riches beyond imagination, one vein from which all others flowed.

Somewhere in this Mother Lode was a lake in a bed of gold, or maybe a wall shimmering in gold.

[Some Californians] are looking for a hidden lake in the mountains called 'Gold Lake,' where the gold is said to exist in great quantities.

—Margaret Frink, 1850

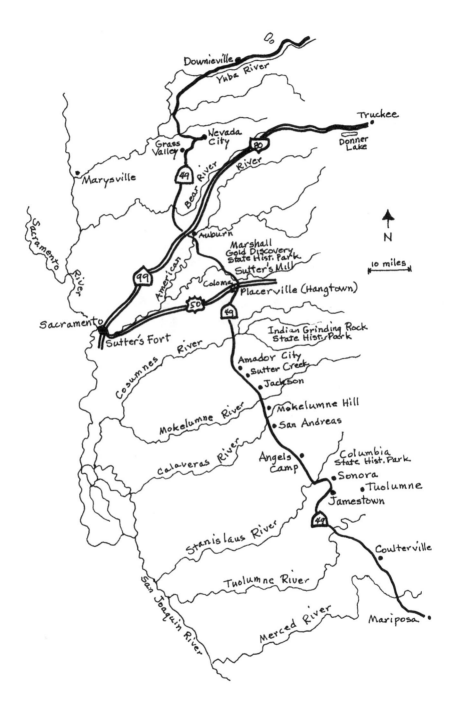

There really was a Mother Lode of gold. But it wasn't a lake or a shining wall. It was a network of veins of gold-laden quartz that reached like blood vessels through the western foothills of the Sierra Nevada. The main vein stretched from Johann Sutter's Mill, east of Sacramento at Coloma, and south to about Mariposa, where John Fremont would strike it rich and then lose it all. Branches from the main lode ran for another 100 miles or so to the north and then eastward toward Nevada. There really was a Mother Lode of gold.

Mexicans from the state of Sonora named the Mother Lode. When they began to arrive in *El Dorado* in the winter of 1848–49, they looked around and saw country like their own *Veta Madre* in Mexico. And so the Mexican *Veta Madre* became the California Mother Lode.

The name California, some say, emerges from tales of an island of gold to the West ruled by dark-skinned Amazons and led by Queen Calafia. The Spanish writer Montalvo spun a tale about the fabled Amazon Queen and her women warriors who had fought halfway around the world on the side of the Turks in the battle for Constantinople.

> **Know ye that on the right hand of the**
> **Indies there is an island called**
> **California, very near the Terrestrial**
> **Paradise, which is peopled with**
> **black women without any men among**
> **them, because they were accustomed**
> **to live after the fashion of the**
> **Amazons. They were of strong and**
> **hardy bodies, of ardent courage and**
> **of great force.**[1]

That's how Montalvo began his yarn starring his chivalric hero, Esplandian, who fought against the Amazons.

> **Their arms were all of gold . . ., for**
> **in all the island there is no other**
> **metal but gold. . . . They had many**
> **ships in which they sailed to other**
> **climes to carry on their forage to**
> **obtain booty . . ..**[2]

From mythical times, the path to Paradise always led westward. Gold has ensnared men and women in its shimmering web for thousands of years, with legends of golden eggs and golden apples, golden rings and statues and temples, lands of gold and paradise—lands always lying to the West.

On his magic ship, the *Argo,* the Greek hero Jason sailed with his Argonauts to find the golden fleece of the magic ram—a myth probably based on the Armenian mode of washing gold from sand with sheepskins. Alchemists of the Middle Ages tried to perform the ultimate magic: making gold from other metals.

Spanish explorers knew the stories of a golden land to the West. Christopher Columbus himself told of women warriors living on an island in the New World. Spanish conquistadors murdered thousands in their path as they grabbed the golden riches of the Aztecs and then turned north to search for the fabled Seven Cities of Cibola.

The gold was there. But the conquistadors never found it. The Americans did, and it made all the difference. The Spanish who came to California marched under the cross and the sword. With soldiers guarding them, Franciscan priests established a chain of Catholic missions, the distance of a day's walk apart, along California's coast. But they never got into the gold country. The padres heard rumors about gold but they didn't want to have anything to do with it. The Spanish let the gold slip right through their fingers.

The California Gold Rush was not simply an outbreak of gold fever. It was a time of breakneck change, a setting where just about anything could happen, and did. It was a carnival, grotesque and whimsical. Its cast of characters included ordinary people there for the show mingling with clowns in garish costumes, masked bandits and outlaws, lost children, vagabonds, painted ladies, gamblers, and hucksters selling goods and dreams.

Whatever fantastic thing you can imagine about the California Gold Rush, it probably happened. But for openers, consider these outrageous facts and figures:

• Between 1848 and 1857, an estimated five hundred million dollars came out of California's Mother Lode—more than any other rush for gold.[3]

• Within two years of the 1848 gold discovery, the non-Indian population of what is now California ballooned from approximately fifteen thousand to ninety-three thousand.[4]

• More than three hundred thousand native people lived in present-day California before Spanish colonization in 1769. By the end of the nineteenth century, the native population was fewer than twenty thousand.[5]

• Indian people, many of them in family groups, were perhaps half the estimated four thousand miners during the summer of 1848.[6]

• In 1849, as many as ninety thousand people, mostly men, arrived in California, traveling by land and sea. By the time they got there, most of the placer gold—surface gold—already was gone.

• California gold seekers spent more than six million dollars on Bowie knives and pistols in the first five years of the Gold Rush.[7]

• Barely a week after the California gold discovery, the Treaty of Guadalupe Hidalgo ended the Mexican war and ceded Alta (upper) California to the US.

Until recently, western women's voices were muted, their experiences all but ignored. No more. Historian Lillian Schlissel pioneered in giving voice to westward women with her 1982 book, *Women's Diaries of the Westward Journey*. Ten years later, JoAnn Levy's *They Saw the Elephant: Women in the California Gold Rush* enhanced Mother Lode lore.

Others, too, have analyzed the history of this amazing time, and its meaning for the women who were there.

So why *Women's Voices from the Mother Lode?* Women's voices have held a fascination for me through more than twenty years of writing, teaching, and speaking. It is a logical continuation of my *Women's Voices* series, beginning with *Women's Voices from the Oregon Trail* (1993) and *Women's Voices from the Western Frontier* (1995). There remain many voices to be heard from the everyday lives of the women who came on this mostly-male journey.

Women's Voices from the Mother Lode—some have spelled it Mother Load, which says it too—is mainly women's stories, though you will hear men's voices too, and children's. And not just the white women who met here, though they are the easiest to find because they were the ones who left written records of their lives. I try to listen for the multicolored voices of the women who met in the Mother Lode country, the Indian women who already were here, and the women who came from every direction.

It is impossible to say how many women participated in the California Gold Rush, because the figures vary wildly depending on the year and the place. But women were here. They always have been here. Moreover, it's dangerous to make generalizations about any group of people during the Gold Rush, including women. Because the Gold Rush is a confusion of contradictions.

"[L]et not the reader fancy that the author has contradicted herself," wrote Eliza Farnham, reformer and observer extraordinaire. She went on to explain:

**It is rather the country, and the life
of it, which are full of contradictions.
To-day is black, tomorrow white. . . .
Thus, life wears on, constant in
nothing but its fluctuations . . ..**

Like a cauldron building up to the boiling-over point, chaos was building in the Mother Lode country even before gold was found. Land once inhabited by Indian people went to Spain, then Mexico, and finally, the US. This book covers the time leading up to the 1848 California gold discovery, and into the 1850s. The decade after the 1848 gold discovery marked the transition from what one author called "anybody's gold"—relatively easy gold—to the era of salaried, company-run mining operations.

I focus mainly on the people of the gold districts of the Mother Lode country. Sometimes, though, I detour from these boundaries of time and place to pick up a good story, or perhaps to make a case.

From 1998 through 2000, California commemorates its Sesquicentennial—the 150th anniversary of the Discovery of Gold (1848–1998), the Gold Rush (1849–1999), and Statehood (1850–2000). Women were here during all of these events. And their voices now are heard.

Listen . . .

MANUELLA'S SONG

I am a fine-looking woman; still I am running with my tears.
—from a
traditional song
(Maidu)[1]

Manuella
*Courtesy Calaveras County Historical
Society, San Andreas, CA*

You say the story begins when Marshall
    reaches for the gold.
You say it begins when the word gold
    forms on his lips.

The story does not begin with the gold.
The story begins with the Grandmother.
All stories begin with the Grandmother.
The one who propelled the earth, the sky, the sea
    and all its creatures
        From the darkness of her womb long ago.

The Grandmother begins and sustains.
The Grandfather builds and protects.

It is all one.
We are all one.

You see me, Manuella, as the Old Indian Woman.
The old one squatting beside the water
    with her pan, looking for gold.
In the water I see the face of an old woman
       Who has known the joy
       of living free on the earth.
It is a joy you will never know.

With your race for gold,
    you have invaded the earth—
      Source of joy and wisdom.

I see the face of an old woman who has known
    the terrors of seeing my people,
      once fiercely strong, now weak and dying.
You say they are gone, vanished.
They are not vanished.
They are dead of disease and violence.

I see the face of an old woman
Banished from the land that once belonged
    to no one and to everyone.
Banished from the land
    where the water running clear was our gold,
And the little acorn, gold of the giant oak.

I see the face of a mighty woman
    Who
        yet
           lives.

I am a fine-looking woman;
    still I am running with my tears.

CHAPTER ONE

Fandango

O-soo mate, the grizzly bear, and Hai-yah-ko, the first people, made the *chaw'se,* mortar holes, in the flat-topped rocks. Then Ned-na-ka ta, the rock maidens made the stone pestles for grinding acorn.

—Miwok legend[1]

On a hot June day, I walked along the path to Indian Grinding Rock at Chaw'se State Park in the heart of Mother Lode country. The grinding rock is a massive, low flat rock in a lovely meadow—donated for a public park by a pioneer descendant so that the land and the memory here would live. In the rock are hundreds of cuplike holes formed by the Maidu women pounding and grinding acorns—their gold from the Mother Lode—with thick rod-shaped stones.

In this quiet place where the oak tree still reaches branches to the sky and sends long roots deep within the earth, I imagined the sounds of the women singing while beating on the rocks in rhythm. I listened for the sounds of children's laughter, wind filtering through the pines, and clear, life-giving water tumbling through the meadow.

I listened to the voice of a park ranger, herself

**Chaw'se,
Indian
Grinding Rock
State
Historic Park,
Pine Grove, CA**

part Maidu, telling of her ancestors' loss of their water as the miners diverted it for their mines, driving the Maidu to higher, unfamiliar ground.

I am told that after the miners began using stamp mills to crush the quartz to get to the gold, you could hear the pounding of the mills through the entire Mother Lode country. No longer could you hear the rhythmic pounding and singing of the women, and the water running clear.

To the Miwok, Maidu, and other peoples of the Mother

Stamp mill, Grass Valley, CA

Lode country, gifts of the earth were of value. Indian people, and Mexicans to follow, knew of gold in their earth. But you couldn't eat gold. It didn't keep you warm in winter. To the people who would come clambering into their country, gold had more value than the land. More value, even, than the lives of the people they found living on the land.

Chet Orloff, Executive Director of the Oregon Historical Society, has described the frontier West as a quick two-step. In the Mother Lode, the mining frontier was a mad dance that whirled the world around and changed everything—a Spanish fandango of crazy rhythms, a slow tango, and then a quick two-step.

In the golden Sierra Nevada foothills, a few wild steps would take a quiet golden land to a state of loud riches and chaos within just a few seasons of the earth. The world known by the Indian people of the Mother Lode had begun to change before the gold discovery. The foothills people had been safe from the Spanish soldiers hunting converts and laborers for the coastal missions. But they were not protected from invasions of refugees and diseases escaping the missions. And they were not safe from diseases brought by foreign trappers and settlers.

In 1823, with Mexican independence from Spain, California became part of Mexico. In 1834, Mexico secularized the missions, which were to have been ceded back to the Indian people, who were to become citizens. Instead of returning to the Indian people, the missions became part of the many land grants ceded mostly to Mexicans, some of them women.

With the transition in governments, the women's names were changed to men's names on the documents, so that Juana became Juan, and Antonia

became Antonio, and so on.² Some land grants went
to foreigners, including Johann Sutter. Like the
Spanish priests had done in their missions, the
Swiss swashbuckler used Indian labor to build his
empire at Sutter's Fort.

Americans and other foreigners began trickling
into California, settling on Mexican land—most of
them illegally. By 1846, President Polk had provoked war with Mexico. It ended with the February
1848 Treaty of Guadalupe Hidalgo, which, as Polk
planned, won for the US Mexican lands, including
Alta California. In an astonishing bit of timing,
James Marshall discovered gold in the Mother Lode
just one week before the US took over California.

By the time the land and sea parade of gold seekers began lurching toward the Mother Lode, land
seekers already had been making their way to
Oregon and California. The westward pilgrims
marched under the banner of what they believed to
be God-given Manifest Destiny, articulated in the
US Congress in 1846: "[O]ur manifest destiny [is] to
spread over this whole continent."³ It meant that

God intended the western lands for the United States. Anyone already there would simply have to get out of the way.

And when in 1848 the Mother Lode of gold revealed herself and all her riches to James Marshall, an American, wasn't that America's Manifest Destiny?

> **We love the glorious western land,**
> **Ho! Westward Ho!**
> **For here the people's hearts expand,**
> **Ho! Westward Ho!**
> **And on the prairies broad and grand,**
> **Ho! Westward Ho!**
> **We all can see Jehovah's hand,**
> **Ho! Westward Ho!**
>
> —traditional westward migration song,
> to be sung reverently

If westward is destiny, that's where you keep moving. Families had moved to Oregon Country and California since the early 1840s, and some even before that. Many of them simply kept moving westward as the US continued to claim land. It was part of the Some Place Else urge that kept people moving onward, where surely things would be better.

The jump to Oregon or California was a big one. Most land between Missouri and the West Coast hadn't yet been taken from the Indians, so there was virtually no place to stop in between, except for a few military and trading posts.

So until the Gold Rush, westward trails were mostly trails to land—land for the family, land to build a new home on, make a new beginning. Land was why the whole family went. Land was why men wanted their wives along, especially going to

Oregon. There, if their timing was right, men could double their land since wives also could claim land.

> so in the spring of 1845 we made
> what preparations we could all of us
> together & started for oragon.   there
> was a great deal of talk about that
> country that we could get homes if
> we would settle on the land & that
> there was a big lot of land for A man,
> & A lot I forget how much for his wife
> & for each child if they would settle
> there   Well we thought that was a
> good thing & away we started very
> poorly suplied in April 1845.
>
> —Eliza Gregson

While the Oregon Trail remained a family trail, the 1849 Gold Rush turned the California trails (there were many) into pretty much male trails. Women—certainly ladies—weren't welcome on the male trails. Too dangerous. Men alone could travel faster to the land of gold. Besides, the gold rush adventure was a temporary thing. The point of it all was to get there as fast as you could, pick up the gold, and come strutting back home, pockets full of gold. Most wives weren't invited until 1852, when men in the Mother Lode realized they needed some company, some help, and some civilizing.

**For the Good time has come at last,
And as we all are told, Sir,
We shall be rich at once now,
With California Gold, Sir.**[4]

Whatever the destination, US law handed over to a husband the right to decide where his family would live—even if it was with his relatives while he headed for the gold. So according to law, it didn't matter where the woman wanted to be. That decision was up to the husband.

But the law didn't stop a lot of women, no matter what their husbands said. Just as countless women refused to go to Oregon, many came to California, whether they were wanted or not.

**I thought where he could go I could,
and where I went I could take my
two little toddling babies.**
                        —Luzena Wilson, 1849

My sense is that more women came willingly, even enthusiastically, to the Mother Lode than to Oregon, mainly because gold rush California didn't look like a permanent move. Because more Mother Lode-bound women were single, or had left their children home, they had more time and freedom to enjoy the adventure. And—they were going for the gold, whether from the gold fields or from the miners' pockets.

**Mrs. McKinney had a nephew who
went to California in 1849, and she
told me wonderful tales of the
abundance of gold that she had
heard; 'that they kept flour-scoops to
scoop the gold out of the barrels that**

they kept it in, and that you could
soon get all that you needed for the
rest of your life. And as for a woman,
if she could cook at all, she could get
$16.00 per week for each man that
she cooks for, and the only cooking
required to be done was just to boil
meat and potatoes and serve them on
a big chip of wood, instead of a plate,
and the boarder furnished the
provisions.' I began at once to figure
up in my mind how many men I
could cook for, if there should be no
better way of making money.

—Margaret Frink, 1850

Knowing that all those men were headed for
California, a lot of women figured they could profit
by selling services, legal or not, ladylike or not.

The miners came in '49
The whores in '51
They rolled around the
    bar room floor
And made a native son.

—popular western ditty

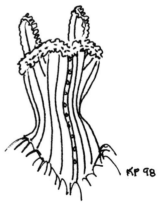

Especially in the early years, "ladies" were greatly outnumbered, not only by men, but by women who made their living "rolling around" with the miners. Many of the latter arrived by ship, and from foreign countries.

I, as the only unmarried young lady in a town of 5,000 inhabitants, was in great demand. . . . Of the five thousand inhabitants of Columbia about twenty-five were women . . . Besides there were about 300 women of the "gold Belt' (the badge of the 'Red Light' women).

—Ellen August Sears, 1855

Women who went West, especially white women, were under the influence of what historian Barbara Welter called "The Cult of True Womanhood." Like their sisters at home, frontier-bound women were expected to think, act and dress as "ladies." No one may have cared about a man's past, but a woman must demonstrate that she was a lady if she wanted respect.

The nineteenth century was a time of global upheaval—land exploration, revolutions, famines, epidemics, wars, and the industrial revolution. Women were to be the models of stability, the ones to hold family and community together and shape society through their "higher" moral example. A True Woman was supposed to be pious, pure, domestic, and submissive. And married. She was to maintain religious traditions, protect her sexual purity, protect her home as a haven for her family, and defer decisions and opinions to her husband, who was, of course, wiser than she in worldly affairs. Wherever she went, she was to bring her civilizing influence.

Many laws and traditions were designed to control women's behavior by not allowing them to speak in public, vote, own property. If married, they were not supposed to keep their own money, dress comfortably, determine the number of births, make their own decisions, or have custody of their children.

In truth, woman, like children, has but one right and that is the right to protection. The right to protection involves the obligation to obey.

—George Fitzhugh, defender of slavery
and the Cult of Domesticity[5]

Even in the West, freedom was supposed to be for men, not for women. But I would venture to say that the codes of True Womanhood were so outrageous that there probably wasn't a woman alive who didn't break them. Yet most women wore the mask of True Womanhood. It was easier. And safer, because women who did not appear to be ladies were vulnerable to attack.

By 1849, the rules and laws were being questioned in public. In Seneca Falls, New York, women had convened the first women's rights convention in the world. It was 1848—months after the gold discovery and before the stampede to the Mother Lode. At Seneca Falls, women and men demanded rights for women ranging from property rights to child custody, and—the most radical of all—the right to vote.

We hold these truths to be self-evident: that all men and women are created equal; that they are endowed by their Creator with certain inalienable rights; that among these are life, liberty, and the pursuit of happiness . . . .

—from the Declaration of Sentiments,
First Women's Rights Convention

In 1851, Amelia Jenks Bloomer began to publicize a costume first worn at Seneca Falls—bloomers. That shocking Turkish trouser-like costume actually allowed women to move freely.

Ladies heading for western lands, some wearing

bloomers, carried with them the seeds of female revolution as well as seeds to plant in the earth. Imagine True Womanhood on the trail. When your child has died of cholera, when your husband insists on taking a dangerous cutoff, when you can barely speak or see because of endless alkali dust, when your clothes are in rags and there's no water even to wash the grime off your face—True Womanhood takes a back road to survival.

If the Cult of True Womanhood prescribed a woman's behavior, the Cult of Domesticity defined her place—the home. Wherever she was, it was the woman's job to do women's work—bear the children and take care of them; do the "dredful wash," as one woman put it; cook, clean—you know the routine. How well she kept her home and the rules determined a woman's status.

Gold rush women broke many of the rules right up front, though most hardly broke free of domestic duties. Traveling as single women, leaving children behind, being in mostly male company—all broke the code. And so, California women got a reputation for being uppity—strong-minded women, they were called.

Being in male territory had its advantages. If a woman was looking for a husband, there were plenty of opportunities to snag one.

> **i tell you the woman are in great**
> **demand in this country no matter**
> **whether they are married or not . . .**
> **there is a first rate Chance for a**
> **single woman   she can have her**
> **choice of thousands**
>
> —Abby Mansur, 1853

Women—white English speaking ladies, that is— were treated as rare jewels, as long as they didn't overstep their bounds too far. Behavior that would have been objectionable in cultured circles was acceptable in mining camps. Still, women were careful to wear their True Woman masks.

True Womanhood, though unrealistic, was a tool for the white majority. Anglo women may have left some of the rules behind, but most never freed themselves from the bonds of classism and racism. No matter how hard a lady had to work, how tattered her clothing, how leaky her roof, she believed that at least she was above women—and men—with dark skin, unladylike women who wore flamboyant clothing and rode horses astride, women who were paid for having sex, and women who lived on the ground and knew how to find and prepare food the earth provided.

> **Woman is beginning to awaken to her true position. . . . It is her province and privilege to disseminate the blessings of purity and peace; and surely in California she can see there is work for her hands to do.**
> —Lorena Hays, Cooks Bar, 1854

It was women's work to bring stability and build community. Even as they began to provide home-baked bread and pie and clean clothes, women also expected men to behave. And as they realized they might stay, they began to initiate schools and churches—the things of community, safety, and home.

The women of the Mother Lode were there for many reasons. Some already lived there. Some came out of sheer stubbornness, some for the adventure, and many others for the gold. Some, like the women of Sonora, Mexico, came with their families. Some, like most Chinese prostitutes, came unwillingly. Some came to escape poverty and even starvation, others to escape slavery and oppression.

Whatever their motive, however they came, none could escape the artificial definitions of what it meant to be a woman. Some still clung to expectations of True Womanhood, and some defied them. Some became rich, and others lost their very lives because they were women.

There were many victories, and many losses. Perhaps the greatest loss was the failure of all people who met in the Mother Lode to listen and to learn from one another, and thus to create something better than any of them had ever known, or ever would know.

CHAPTER TWO

The Mother Lode Awakens

It was some time before we could believe it was real gold.

—Eliza Gregson, 1848

Eliza Gregson was among the land seekers who trekked overland to the Mother Lode country before the gold discovery. It was only through the whimsy of fortune and human folly that she and her family landed here at the time of the gold discovery in the Mother Lode. Eliza, whose movable life had taken her halfway around the world, was an eyewitness to the slap-dash events that led up to the discovery of gold, and the rush that followed.

Eliza wrote her story because she wanted others to know about the lives of pioneer women, and about her own search for riches. And perhaps to tell us what riches really are.

Her hopeful childhood in England turned upside down when the gambling monster grabbed her father and stole all of his family's money, propelling him "by the underground railroad for America." Eliza was twelve when she watched her family's belongings auctioned off, including their precious blankets. For three years, she and her brothers worked fifteen-hour days in a cotton factory, existing on "sometimes milk & other times

treakle [treacle—molasses] & oat meal much [mush]
3 times a day."

Then came the family's voyage across the
Atlantic to America, paid for by her father; her marriage at age nineteen; her parents' divorce; the birth
of a child; epidemics of malaria and other diseases
that plagued the whole family and took the baby;
and several moves westward. The last move west
wasn't even supposed to be to California. The family—by now Eliza and her husband, and her mother,
brother, and sisters—"started for oragon" in 1845.

But they never made it to Oregon. Near Fort
Hall, they met up with "Old Man" Caleb
Greenwood, who offered the emigrants food, supplies, and land on behalf of Johann Sutter if they
would choose to go to California.

A hot discussion followed. Which way to go?
Those for Oregon pointed out that since Mexico
claimed California, there was no guarantee of land.
Americans would be in a foreign country, and might
get mixed up in a war with Mexico. Besides, the

Fort Hall replica, Pocatello, ID

emigrants would only be helping Sutter promote his land schemes.

Caleb Greenwood argued that Indians were more dangerous on the Oregon Trail; the road to California was better. They could take up more land in California, and the climate was sublime, with plenty of hunting and fishing.[1]

**Old
Parting of the
Ways Monument,
South Pass, WY**

And so, whimsy turned Eliza and her family toward California.

Greenwood was wrong about the Indians, the road, and the land. The rest still is debatable. The truth was, there was no road to California; it was only a primitive path through largely untried country. And "the indians were very bad," Eliza Gregson remembered. They killed most of her family's cattle.

The journey was harder than Eliza could have imagined.

> **our cattle was giving out so we had to**
> **cut the wagon down & make a cart of**
> **it & throw away some of our goods**
> **things began to look very scaly just**
> **then . . . .**

Eliza and the others trudged on foot through the notorious Forty Mile Desert, in present-day Nevada, and the rest of the way into the Mother Lode country.

. . . at last we came to the Sierra Navada Mountains which seemed insurmountable . . . Well we still kept up the march day after day, ever watching and looking for the promised land. At length we arrived at . . . Sutters fort on the Sacramento river.

It was October 1845. In "the promised land," Eliza Gregson's family started again "trying in all ways to make a liveing." Captain Sutter came through with provisions and help, but Eliza's family never got their promised land. California still was Mexican territory and Eliza's family were considered trespassers. As the Oregonians had predicted, they got mixed up in the war between Mexico and the US.

Sutter's Fort State Historic Park, Sacramento, CA

> **when we arrived at the fort   the**
> **governor of Call* [Pio Pico] sent a**
> **written document to Cap Sutter**
> **Autherizeing him to drive back the**
> **americans & not to let them stop in**
> **the country.   well most of the**
> **emigrants had but very little of**
> **anything left & it was out of the**
> **question.   we could not & would not**
> **leave.**

Eliza Gregson's family did not leave. Between various jobs at and near Sutter's Fort, James Gregson became involved in several skirmishes with Mexicans, quickly followed by the war with Mexico.

All this time, Eliza stayed at the fort, "trying all ways to make a liveing."

---

*Eliza's abbreviation for California.

Replica of Sutter's Mill
Marshall Gold Discovery State Historic Park, Coloma, CA

**there was no work for woman
excepting a little cooking & very little
at that.   & our cloathes we had to
patch untill the original peice could
scarcely be found.   our men worked
for 1 dollar per day. & common dress
goods $1 per yard.   so it took $8 to
buy 1 dress & our food was very
coarse flour & sometimes pretty good
beef   no coffee or tea or sugar or
Milk or butter.**

Ever the keen observer, Eliza watched a panorama of history and its actors pass by in their sometimes tragic, sometimes comic dance of life. One of the leading characters in this drama was "Captain" Johann Sutter.

Sutter had made a little empire for himself near the confluence of the American and Sacramento Rivers, where Sacramento would quickly grow. Exploiting the labor of local Indian people like the mission padres before him, Sutter had built a forti-

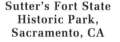

**Sutter's Fort State
Historic Park,
Sacramento, CA**

fication and reigned over a sizeable trade and farming operation. A man with ample ego, Sutter often said, "I am no ordinary gentleman, no Sir. I am an extraordinary gentleman, yes Sir, I am. I strive to be honored. I will do anything for honor."[2]

Many of the emigrants who found shelter and jobs at his settlement owed their lives to the flamboyant Swiss. "[T]he old Cap was very generous to a fault," Eliza Gregson remembered. "[S]o large was his heart that he could not say no . . . ."

One of the first to receive a Mexican land grant while California still was Mexican, "Captain" Sutter (a title he gave himself) had deserted his family, along with sizeable debts in Switzerland, to build the empire he called "New Helvetia."

Like virtually all the white settlers, Eliza viewed the "wild digers" (Indian people) at the fort as "degraded" and inferior. So it's little wonder that Eliza saw nothing wrong with the way the Indians received their food at Sutter's Fort.

> **they were fed on boiled bran
> sometimes a few beef bones thrown in
> their food was put into long wooden
> troughs & laid on the ground & the
> indians would sit on each side of the
> trough & scupe their mess with thier
> hands. & it was laughable to see them
> When it was two hot they would
> shake their hands.**

At a time and place where there seemed to be nothing wrong with stealing Indian children as virtual slaves, Eliza recalled a man who "had one little indian boy about 9 or 10 years old   he used to vent his bad temper on the little fellow.   the boy used to run & cling to me for procection [protection] after a week or two the boy ran away & was not seen again."

When an epidemic of Sacramento fever (presumably malaria) attacked Eliza, her husband and child, she observed that "the indians suffered tererable they died almost in heaps & was not able one to bury the other when he died."

Like many women both on the frontier and back in "the States," Eliza often was left to fend for herself. The winter after her first child was born was "a very wet one & we were scarce of food and fuel and we had hard work to keep fires."

> **Well [James] went & left me & my little girl about six weeks old. to do [the] best I could. I got along pretty well untill nearly Christmass with nothing to do only take care of the little one, the worst of it [was] I had very little to eat & I got so thin in flesh that I could scarsely carry the few cloaths that were on my back. I was nursing a fat cross baby & had very little norishments—about that time Mrs leahy she says to me come & live with me & we will put our grub together it will be better for us both, as her husband was gone to so I moved the few things I had & stayed with her & Mrs Montgomery.**

"Mrs. Montgomery" was Sarah Armstrong Montgomery, who had arrived at Sutter's Fort in the spring of 1845, about the time Eliza left for "oragan." Nineteen-year-old Sarah was in the Stephens-Townsend-Murphy party, the first to bring wagons across the Sierra Nevada. Hers was a journey that stretched into an entire year, ending with a macabre dance with time, weather, and luck.

Sarah was one of several women and children left stranded in the mountains in December while a rescue party made its way to Sutter's Fort to bring back supplies and food. Incredibly, when the rescuers reached the fort, intent on getting help, Sutter ordered them instead to go fight in one of his skirmishes with Mexicans. The rescuers finally started back six weeks after they had left the trapped travelers. Miraculously, not a life was lost, and the stranded band even increased by two souls with the birth of two babies in the mountains.

Sarah Montgomery made history in 1846 by hosting the first known quilting party in California. Eliza may have attended the quilting, but didn't mention the event in her reminiscences.

Captain Sutter himself noted the event:

> **To day was a quilting at Montgomeris, the whole Neighborhood was invited, and a great many was there present, I keept house and let go nearly all the Gentlemen.**[3]

Sarah Montgomery would go on to have her own dance with luck and whimsy.

Her first husband, Allen Montgomery, deserted her. Her second husband was a known "scoundrel," and her third turned out to be a thief and a bigamist. But, California-style, Sarah Armstrong Montgomery Green Wallis would turn tragedy on its head and go on to become the owner of a farm and a leading suffragist. And she would make and lose a fortune.

Back at Sutter's Fort, the women huddled in the cold and looked after their families while their men were off to the war with Mexico.

In the miserable early winter of 1847, Eliza witnessed the arrival of the remains of the Donner party—those who survived the most infamous and grotesque journey to California.

Donner Lake looking toward the Sierra Nevada.
Photo by Hanne Gwilym

This is a tale, sadly true, of extreme courage and heroism, villainy and stupidity. And, most of all, stark, paralyzing fear. The party had been stranded for months near Truckee (now Donner) Lake [CA], unable to cross the mountains. Nearly half the eighty-one who were trapped had died of cold and starvation. Many of the living ultimately survived on the flesh of those who had died. They died because they lingered too long on the trail, and took an untried cutoff at the urging of Lansford Hastings. This cavalier fellow had not traveled the route with wagons, nor was he there to guide the ill-fated party, as promised.

Among the heroes were women and men who helped others survive, and men who risked their lives to rescue the survivors. Two of the heroes were would-be rescuers, Indians from Fort Sutter who were murdered and eaten by two crazed survivors.

The memory of the survivors' arrival at Sutter's Fort remained starkly clear in Eliza's memory:

> **I shall never forget the looks of those**
> **people for the most part of them were**
> **crazey & their eyes danced &**
> **sparkled in their heads like stars.**

Eliza marveled at stories she heard about women's courage during their ordeal:

> **the wemen would take the lead over**
> **the snow & beat the track for the men**
> **to walk in. but for all that the men**
> **sunk down & died.   the wemen even**
> **led them by the hand & made the**
> **camp fires & gave them food . . . . So**
> **speak about womens rights   say they**
> **are weak & ought to have no rights**

Questions of heroism, cowardice, and villainy among the members of the Donner Party have yet to be settled. But one thing is known: three-fourths of the women, two-thirds of the children, and only one-third of the men survived.

Writer and reformer Eliza Farnham believed that more women and children survived because of women's supposed moral superiority, and because most were in family groups, while many of the men traveled alone. One of the heroes was Charles Stanton, a single man who made it to Sutter's Fort and brought back food and supplies to Donner Lake. He froze to death trying to bring some of the survivors over the mountain.

James Frazier Reed wrote in his diary about a place now called Flowery Lake, south of present-day Wells, Nevada:

Left the Basin Camp or Mad Womens Camp as all the women were mad with anger . . . .[4]

The women were angry because their voices were not heard, not until all of them together faced cold death.

Perhaps the smartest advice from the whole horrible episode came from thirteen-year-old Virginia Reed.

never take no cutofs and hury along as fast as you can

Donner memorial, on the site of the Breen cabin, used by members of the Donner party. The memorial stands at the height reached by the snow that winter, and bears an odd inscription: "Virile to risk and find kindly withal and a ready help facing the brunt of fate. Indomitable— unafraid."
Donner Memorial State Park, Truckee, CA

Donner party survivors were the most desperate of all the emigrants to arrive at Sutter's Fort. But there were other visitors, and sickness was one of the most frequent.

James Gregson suffered from malaria and scurvy. At one point he was near death and the doctor, though he collected his fee, could do nothing for him. Poorer and with her husband no nearer to recovery, Eliza sat down and thought. And, like many frontier women, she turned to Mother Nature.

**Then I went out in the fields. I could
find nothing no not even a blade of
grass. All that there was, was some
cow manure and it came to me, the
cows have eaten up all the grass and
herbs, why not the manure make a
good medicine. So I took some of it
wrapped it up in a cloth and boiled it
then I filled a pint bowl full and took
it to him. When he saw it he said,
You want to poison me. I told him no
see me drink. with that he took the
bowl with both hands and drank it
all and went to sleep.   slept 3 or 4
hours but the fever was gone . . . . my
husband recovered his health partly
but not fully for a long time.**

In her reminiscences in old age, Eliza Gregson
claimed that Captain Sutter sent her and her husband to Coloma, the site of the new sawmill, in late
1847. James was to be a blacksmith and Eliza was to
cook. Yet there is no record of the couple having
lived there at that time. Some scholars speculate
that Eliza fudged on the truth a bit in order to place
herself in the middle of the event that caught the
world on fire: the discovery of gold at Sutter's Mill.

In the foothills of the Sierra Nevada, the dry
land hosts pine and oak and chaparral. Icy streams
flow westward from mountain lakes to the rich
lands of the valleys below.

In this place near the Nisenan village of Ko-lo-
ma (later known as Coloma), James Marshall was in
charge of building a sawmill for Johann Sutter. On a
January morning in 1848, something glowed and
winked at James Marshall in the millrace. Golden
fantasies must have flashed through his mind.

Gold discovery site, American River
Marshall Gold Discovery State Historic Park, Coloma, CA

Real gold? Or fools' gold?

He picked up a flake of the stuff. Then another. He dug around a bit and gathered up more pieces. This is real gold, he thought.

James Marshall remembered stories of mysterious early Indian tribes said to have "dwelt on this continent centuries ago, and built those cities and temples, the ruins of which are scattered about this solitary wilds."[5] Maybe this is gold hidden away by these long-ago Indians, he mused. But it seemed to be all around.

"Hey, boys, by God I believe I've found a gold mine," he announced to some of the mill workers. Naw—it's only fool's gold, some of them muttered, chortling to themselves about this dreamer who believed in magic.

James showed a piece to Elizabeth Jane Wimmer—Jennie, she was called. Jennie, who came from gold country in Georgia, was there at the mill cooking and doing laundry for her Mormon family and the workers. She tossed the pebble into her soap kettle. If it was gold, she knew, it wouldn't melt, but would sink to the bottom and still be there the next morning.

Next morning, "there was my gold as bright as it could be."[6]

James Marshall took off for Sutter's Fort. Johann Sutter wasn't expecting the handful of golden grains his mill foreman flung on his desk. Secretly, the two men studied up on gold, made some tests, and pronounced it—real.

Forebodings surged through Captain Sutter's mind. Indians had told him there was gold in this country—and that it belonged to a demon who guarded his gold-rimmed mountain lake. Gold was bad medicine, they warned.

Visions flashed before him—visions of losing all he had because of gold. His workers would leave to search for gold. Hordes of goldseekers would trample his fields and run off his stock. He had no legal right to the Indian land where the mill stood, so he couldn't claim the gold for himself. So he urged Marshall to keep the discovery quiet.

The Indians were right. For Johann Sutter, gold would turn out to be bad medicine.

The stage was set for the next dizzying two-step in the country of the Mother Lode: the rush for the gold. Surely Johann Sutter and James Marshall knew that gold couldn't be kept secret for long. Someone was going to catch wind of it and light a fire. But even after the secret was out, it smoldered for a while.

In March, the *Californian* newspaper quietly reported the find.

CALIFORNIAN

SAN FRANCISCO, MARCH 15, 1848

GOLD MINE FOUND.—In the newly made raceway of the Saw Mill recently erected by Captain Sutter, on the American Fork, gold has been found in considerable quanti- ties. One person brought thirty dollars worth to New Helvetia, gathered there in a short time. California, no doubt, is rich in mineral wealth, great changes here for scientific capi- talists. Gold has been found in almost every part of the country.

The men wondered and talked, and the women too; but neither believed. The sibyls were less skeptical; they said the moon had, for several nights, appeared not more than a cable's length from the earth; that a white raven had been seen playing with an infant; and that an owl had rung the church bells.

—The Reverend Walter Cotton[7]

It turned out to be Sam Brannon who lit the fire. His own San Francisco newspaper first had ignored, then ridiculed the stories of gold, calling the discovery a "superb take-in as was ever got up to guzzle the gullible."[8] Sam decided to check it out himself. Sure enough, there was gold. Lots of gold!

Here was a fantastic opportunity for a man to sell all kinds of goods and paraphernalia to the thousands who surely would be streaming into the foothills for gold. Sam Brannon was the man. Picture him running through the sleepy seaside village of San Francisco waving a bottle of gold dust and yelling "Gold! Gold! Gold from the American River!" To which he added that he had a fine supply of picks and pans for sale.

That's all it took to set off the first wave of the Gold Rush. The *Californian* now loudly proclaimed:

> **The whole country from San Francisco to Los Angeles and from the seashore to the base of the Sierra Nevada resounds with the sordid cry of gold! Gold! Gold!!! while the field is left half-planted, the house half-built, and everything neglected but the manufacture of shovels and pickaxes, and the means of transportation to the spot.[9]**

Meanwhile, back at Sutter's Mill at Coloma, Eliza claimed that "our liveing was very poor."

Soon, Eliza's life turned upside down, along with everyone else's at Sutter's Mill, which wasn't even finished yet.

Menu
AT SUTTER'S MILL
RIGHT AFTER THE GOLD DISCOVERY

- salt beef, poor & salty, looks like blue flint

- salt Salmon too salty & oily that it was not fit to eat

- boild barley

- sometimes boiled wheat & peas dried

- neither bread or Coffee or tea or sugar

- 1 keg of Butter strong enough to run away of itself

about this time gold hunters began to arive with pans & in A short time the new[s] began to spread far & wide

Gold! Gold in California! The news traveled south to Mexico, west to the Sandwich Islands (Hawaii), north to Oregon, and then to Chile and Peru. By summer, Jason-like argonauts came questing for gold from all directions, except from the East. Thousands of Oregonians, some who had pleaded family obligations to avoid military service, dropped what they were doing and headed south. By the end of 1848, perhaps ten thousand gold-seekers had swarmed into the Mother Lode.[10]

Like Argos of the ancient times, I'll leave this modern Greece;

I'm going to California Mines,
To find the golden fleece.

Oh California!
That's the land for me,
I'm going to California
The gold dust for to see.

     —to be sung with gusto
    to the tune of "Oh Susannah"

now the people were coming in from
all parts of . . . Call & chili & by & by
the oragononians commencing to
arive early in the gold excitement
Mr Gregson made the first pick &
afterwards made a good many picks
& drills for the miners. & the men
stopt working on the mill every
thing was gold crazy run away
salors and solders came into the
mines my mother & two brothers &
my sister came to hunt for gold. . . .

In 1848. goods began to arive in the
mines & every kind was very high
prised flour $1 per pound. Coffee
$10 per pound tea $18 per pound &
other things in proporsion eggs $18
per dozen. $1. yard for common
calico. We wemen folks took in all
the sewing such as makeing overalls
We could make $10 per day. . . . but
salt & bad living so long began to tell
on my husband & little girl they
were both taken sick & no one knew
what was the matter

The Gregsons never did strike it rich. They moved to Sonoma, searching for Some Place Else where they would be healthier. The family kept expanding and "trying all ways to make a liveing." James worked in the mines when he wasn't sick, and Eliza washed and sewed and toiled "as best I could."

The golden dream was as slow to awaken in the rest of the world as it was in California. In the summer of 1848, while "every thing was gold crazy" in California, reports of the gold discovery traveled eastward, but newspapers didn't print them. The US State Department even ignored a messenger, believed to be Kit Carson, with a personal dispatch from the US Consul in California.

On August 19, the New York *Herald* reported the gold discovery—by now eight months old. No reaction.

It was none other than President Polk who finally lit the fire. Suddenly he saw a golden opportunity to justify the recent war that had wrested southwestern lands from Mexico, and to bring Americans by the thousands to occupy the newly-won lands. Just as the President was leaving office, here was his chance to go down in history as the one who opened the way for Americans to the riches of California.

As December snows fell in the California gold country, President Polk reported in his State of the Union message that there was gold in California in quantities that would "scarcely command belief." There was so much gold it would pay for the Mexican war 100 times over!

Two days later, another personal dispatch arrived from California: nearly four thousand dollars worth of gold from the Mother Lode packed in a tea caddy. Soon, gold was gleaming on display for all to see in—of all places—the War Department.

Finally, the Eastern Seaboard woke up with a shout that echoed around the world. The wild fandango began, and gold fever spread through the country and a world already infected with disease, poverty and desolation. In February, the forty-niners began to arrive, first by ship, then by land from the east. By the end of 1849, as many as one hundred thousand feverish argonauts had swarmed into California.

In one of history's greatest ironies, by the time most of the forty-niners got there, much of the easy gold was gone.

As for the one who officially started all the excitement, James Marshall basked in telling and retelling his gold discovery story. Soon he was in demand as a guide with special "powers of divination" to find the Mother Lode, which he believed to be a mountain of "golden pebbles."

Marshall never found his mountain, nor did he strike it rich. Neither did Johann Sutter, whose forebodings came true. Both men died in poverty.

In the beginning, anybody with a few simple tools could go for the gold and probably find some, even get rich. It was, as author Joseph Henry Jackson wrote, Anybody's Gold. Poor man's gold. The placer gold—surface gold—could be scraped out of rock with a knife or a spoon. The Sonorans from Mexico taught gringos how to use *bateas* (bowls) to wash and separate the gold flakes,

Placer mining techniques
Courtesy California State Library

nuggets, and dust from sand and gravel. Miners teamed up to "rock" and sift the gold from the gravel in simple contraptions called cradles and long toms.

But soon the easy gold was gone, and most who had come all this way by land or sea to find their own fortunes and make their own wealth could be only wage earners, working for strangers in a strange land. Now, it was mainly big mining companies that could get the capital to do the digging and tearing necessary to get to the gold.

In their mad headlong rush for the gold, they tore into the earth. They took the water flow and changed its direction, tore up the beds where the water flowed and turned it into mud. As they developed more sophisticated methods of getting at the gold, they tore gashes into mountains, reduced hillsides to rubble, coaxed the gold with chemicals, pounded rocks to smithereens, then dug deep into the earth—in some places as far as two miles!

In one strange year, quiet wonderings had turned into a yell heard around the world, a cry that turned lives upside down as wanderers in search of their fortune swarmed to the golden land called California.

And the world never would be the same.

Hydraulic operation at McSorley Pit, Chili Gulch
Courtesy Calaveras County Historical Society, San Andreas, CA

CHAPTER THREE

Dreams for Sale

And the march of men,
and the drift of ships,
And the dreams of fame,
and desire for gold,
They shall go for aye,
as a tale that is told . . .

—from "Isles of the Amazons"
by Joaquin Miller

President Polk boasted over his tea caddy of gold before the world. Suddenly the dream was everywhere—in songs, theatres, newspapers, homes, barber shops, churches, and bars. Fortune tellers had a booming business. And fast-talking salesmen appeared on street corners—selling the dream.

Suddenly there were golden dreams for sale.

Step right up, folks!
Buy your dreams right here!
There's gold in California!
Riverbeds of gold! Mountains of gold!
Stones of shining gold just waiting to be picked up and plunked in your pocket!

And I've got all the stuff you need
to get there and strike it rich.

So step right up, folks! Get your
dreams right here!

Here's a guidebook to show you
where you're goin'.

Right here are your pistols and
bowie knives for fightin' off critters
and tricksters.

To make your trip there just
dandy, whether by land or sea,

Here's your authentic, home-baked
California gingerbread!

Guaranteed to keep good in any
climate for a whole year!

And if you get to feelin' lower
than a snake's belly on the way,

Perk right up with Mrs. Frazier's
Compound Vegetable Cough Remedy!

And for when you get there and
find your gold—

Here's your very own personal
genuine patented gold washer!

Guaranteed to give you the
cleanest gold in California!

So step right up, folks!

Buy your dreams right here!

Many threads wove the dream, and there were plenty of buyers. Never mind if the stories of the gold weren't all true.

Most of the dreamers were men. Some were women.

> **One good old lady . . . declared that she had been dreaming of gold every night for several weeks, and that it had so frustrated her simple household economy that she had relieved her conscience by confessing to her priest—'Absolve me, father, of that sinful dream.'**
>
> —The Reverend Walter Cotton, 1848[2]

In a world already infected with Oregon Fever, Gold Rush Fever was even more virulent.

> **The gold excitement spread like wildfire, even out to our log cabin in the prairie, and as we had almost nothing to lose, and we might gain a fortune, we early caught the fever.**
>
> —Luzena Stanley Wilson, 1849

It really was a fever. "Fevers were common in the nineteenth century, and 'fever' describes what gold did to people," says Thomas Frye, Director of the California Gold Rush Sesquicentennial and Chief Curator Emeritus of History, Oakland Museum of California. "Gold fever became a frenzy, a raging compulsion.

"Here was an opportunity for wealth; it could change people's lives. At home, there was not much opportunity to rise above what a person was born into. Here, you had a chance to become wealthy.

The gold was free—if you could get to where it was."

The fever became a parade of frenzied marchers coming from every direction, bound to "see the elephant" (trail lingo for "been there, done that"). Think of a carnival or a circus parade—a celebration, with boisterous barkers, coaxing you to join the fun. The parade captains lead the way and try to keep order. Following the leaders are all kinds of characters. There are the clowns and tricksters and downright liars, wearing gaudy clothes and masks of comedy and tragedy. They try to make you laugh and often make you cry.

There are animals large and small—dogs and cats, cows and elephants, some scary and snarly, some cuddly. And working through the crowd are the thieves, ready to reach into your pockets when you're not looking.

This is the greatest animal show that we have seen.

—Helen Carpenter, 1857

Accompanying the parade is a riot of sounds—people yelling, dogs barking, chickens cackling, wagons creaking, and the band, with its cornets and fiddles, and drummers pounding out the rhythm, punctuated with occasional gunshots.

This particular parade is a very long one. Sometimes the people argue with the captains and go a different way, and some of them get lost. Some get bored and quiet. Sometimes their costumes and shoes wear out and they have to dress in tatters and go barefoot. And if this parade is by water, the ship itself can catch a fever, grow hot and burn, and sink into the depths.

And yet, it keeps coming—this parade of thousands, coming for the gold.

It's no wonder that gold fever was so lethal. Other fevers festered around the world—cholera, diphtheria, malaria, and tuberculosis. Famine already had killed millions in Ireland alone, and raged through much of Europe and into Russia. This was the time of Dickens' London, seething with poverty, slums, exploitation, and pollution. Revolutions, largely inspired by publication of Karl Marx's *Communist Manifesto,* spread through Europe and beyond. Financial depression, epidemics, and debt roamed the States, especially in its heartland. Hard times stole people's money and put them in debt.

> It was a period of National hard
> times and we being financially
> involved in our business interests
> near Clinton, Iowa, longed to go to
> the new El Dorado and 'pick up' gold
> enough with which to return and pay
> off our debts.
> —Catherine Haun, 1849

> Brokers are all breaking,
>   Credit is all cracked,
> Women all expanding,
>   As the banks contract . . ..
> —from "Hard Times,"
> to be sung to a Schottische, with humor

Here before them was an opportunity to run away from hard times, and maybe strike it rich. What could they lose?

But amid the excitement, some voices preached of Sodom and Gomorrah, and enlisted mothers and wives to stop the madness, cure the fever.

> Mothers and wives! Heed my words!
> Your sons and husbands
> Who follow the siren song of gold
> Are marching straight into the
>   jaws of hell!
> The road to gold is the trail to hell!
>
> Though you are daughters of Eve,
> And bear the stain of original sin,
> You, mothers and wives,
> Must stop this fever raging

through the land!
The road to gold is the trail to hell!

Once they get to that evil land—
    if they ever do—
They will be led to dens of iniquity:
Painted ladies! The wheel of fortune!
And demon rum!
The road to gold is the trail to hell!

Pestilence and starvation
    will follow them.
And if they end up in a tomb of gold,
Their deaths will be a
    burden upon your heart!
Mothers and wives,
    keep your men and boys home!
The road to gold is the trail to hell!

Many who followed the road to gold did indeed fall prey to the evils the preachers warned about. The mothers' pleading and lovers' entreating and even threats of hell and damnation could not stop the fever. And so, the parade to gold left in its wake hopes, debts, doubts, fractured families, broken hearts, and healthy heaps of skepticism.

In Oregon alone, at least two out of three able-bodied Oregon men took off for California gold. Imagine taking your home with you for two thousand miles across plains and mountains and deserts to build a new life, only to have your husband up and take off for the gold and leave you there among strangers in the rain and mud. So many families were disrupted that orphanages grew to take care of children with no place to go.

If they left regrets and unhappy relatives and friends behind, the argonauts had the dream of gold, and it propelled them on. No one—man, woman, or child—was immune to the disease. Sons left parents. Mothers left children. Husbands left wives.

David and Rachel Ann Brown were a black couple living in Ohio who, like thousands of others, believed they could improve their lives with the gold David would bring back from California. He followed his dream in 1852. We can only imagine Rachel's despair to see him go, her fear that she may never see him again.

In her first letter to David after learning of his safe arrival in the northern mining camp of Downieville, Rachel wrote, "I hope for the better. I would like to have you home for I am very lonely without you." She described doing laundry, raising pigs, and other hard work, and urged him to send money to a Mr. Turner (presumably to pay off a debt).

Only two of Rachel's letters survive, and none of his. In her last surviving letter three years after David left, Rachel wrote wistfully:

> **My dear husband, if you had your**
> **business arrainged so you could come**
> **home I would be glad so we could get**
> **fix to housekeep. If you had I do**
> **think that if we could get a place**
> **improved it would be better . . ..**[3]

David stayed in Downieville, and the two never saw each other again.

> **You are going o'er the mountains,**
> **far away from your poor Dine;**
> **I hope you'll ne'er forget the love**
> **of her you leave behind.**
> **Oh, I will dream of thee,**
> **my love, wherever you may be,**
> **The tears will flow into my eyes**
> **when I think of you, dear Joe.**
> —from "Dine and Joe,"
> to be sung dreamily

David Brown joined the parade, along with Irish cotters, European peasants, Basque shepherds, Mexican miners, Cornish miners, Australian adventurers, French bakers, Midwestern farmers, Eastern bankers, prostitutes and professionals and debtors from everywhere, and wives who refused to be left behind.

> **Oh I come from Salem City**
> **With my washbowl on my knee.**
> **I'm going to California,**
> **The gold dust for to see.**

Oh California,
That's the land for me.
I'm going to Sacramento
With my washbowl on my knee.

—Gold Rush theme song,
a parody of Stephen Foster's "Oh Susannah"

By the thousands they came. In 1849, eighty thousand or more gold seekers headed for California. It's hard to tell how many women were among the forty-niners. Some say two percent were women, while others say ten percent or more. Take your pick. Even census figures don't tell the whole story because the census didn't count children or Indian people, and often didn't count prostitutes.

Nearly half the forty-niners came by sea. Westward seafarers sailed from the Eastern seaboard or from Europe thousands of miles around Cape Horn, or the shorter route across Panama or Nicaragua. Others sailed northward from "down under," eastward from Asia and Pacific islands, and southward from Oregon.

Rich and poor and in-between took the sea route. There were rich men, single women, and married couples who had left children behind. There were prospectors backed by investors, single men who had invested their family's life savings in this wild venture, and prostitutes and indentured servants who hoped to pay back the entrepreneurs who footed their fare. Both ladies and prostitutes were more likely to travel by sea than by land.

There was hilarity and dancing and boredom on board, terrible food or no food, and sumptuous banquets. Especially in 1849, some ships were so crowded, it looked as though they would sink any minute under the weight.

**We lived like hogs penned up to fat,
Our vessel was so small.
We had a "duff"⁴ but once a month,
And twice a day a squall.
A meeting now and then was held
Which kicked up quite a stink;
The Captain damned us fore and aft
And wished the box would sink.**

—from "Coming Round the Horn"

Mrs. D.B. Bates' 1850 journey around the Horn took her on several "boxes," but none of them sank—not while she was on them. Hers was the kind of adventure only a novelist with a wild imagination could have dreamed up. But it was true.

Most of the ships carried cargos of coal which tended to catch fire, even on the ocean. The first ship, commanded by her husband, encountered a raging storm while it smoldered for twelve days, and then caught fire. Mrs. Bates watched the flames ignite the hatch and then the mast-head. Clutching her pet goat, she escaped with the other passengers to a long boat just in time to watch the ship turn to a "burning mass upon the water."

A passing ship rescued the shaken travelers and transferred them to another ship. To reach it, they had to climb ropes in the midst of another storm. This ship too carried coal, but the captain assured the passengers that "there was no danger whatever of the *Fanchon's* burning, she was so well ventilated." It was on Christmas Day that Mrs. Bates smelled the by-now familiar odor of coal gas, which turned out again to be smoldering coal. For days, the crew searched for land, scuttling the ship in a Peruvian bay—two hours before it burst into flames.

After a "thrilling adventure" among the Indians, our heroine boarded another ship, which stayed cool, and made it to Panama. With relief, she at last boarded a ship bound for San Francisco.

She must have thought she was dreaming one night when shouts of "Fire! Fire!" woke her up. The other ladies screamed and rushed for the deck. Not Mrs. Bates. She calmly stopped to put on her shoes and stockings. "[H]aving been so often subjected to the fiery ordeal during that eventful year, I had learned to expect it as a matter of course," she wrote.

When she finally arrived in the port of San Francisco nearly a year after she started, Mrs. Bates watched a passenger who had sailed to meet her miner husband. When they found each other in the mad crowd at the wharf, he gazed at her invitingly and asked, "Why don't you kiss me, Bessy?" Searching his bearded face, she responded, "I can't find any place."

Twenty-year-old Ellen August Sears, a single teacher, came by way of Panama in 1855, when she could cross part of the Isthmus by rail. Her "delightful" trip would have lost some of its charm had she known that her ship was leaking the entire journey, and may have gone to a "watery grave" without constant bailing.

Eliza Farnham, a strong-minded widow, had planned to bring a shipload of ladies to tame the wild gold country, but her scheme fizzled. She set sail anyway, bound for California around the Horn with her two young sons. When she dared to demand that passengers be provided good water during the voyage, the annoyed captain tricked her into disembarking. When she returned to get on board, she watched the ship leave—with her sons. Months later, Eliza finally caught up with her sons, whom she found under the care of a woman she had met on the ship.

At the dawn of the Gold Rush, many seafarers left for the Mother Lode in late 1848, beating out those who came by land. Overlanders had to wait for the ground to thaw and the grass to grow in the spring of '49. Then the Gold Rush stampede by land began.

Most overlanders traveled the Oregon-California Trail, which headed west from various "jumping-off places" in the Midwest, and branched off toward California beginning at South Pass and Fort Bridger, in present-day Wyoming. Other overland routes led to the Mother Lode from points farther south, such as the Santa Fe Trail. More than forty thousand crossed the trails in 1849, and even more in 1852, when the Oregon-California Trail once more became a family trail.

To hear most people tell it, preparations for the overland journey took months. Clothing and the wagon cover must be sewn, food and belongings packed, beasts of burden bought and trained, property sold.

The longer the emigrants intended to stay, the more they seemed to pack, though many women bound for the Mother Lode often packed in a weekend.

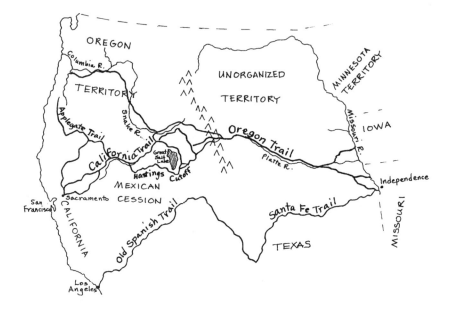

Forty-four-year-old Margaret Frink was one Californian who packed as though she intended to stay. She and her husband began preparing in December 1849 for their journey from Indiana in 1850. They would take with them an eleven-year-old boy who had lived with them for four years, and a twenty-one-year-old man whose parents entrusted him to the Frinks.

Margaret Frink described a comfortable, well-designed wagon "designed expressly for the trip, it being built light, with everything planned for convenience." Green fabric with pockets lined the wagon, and under the floor were compartments and cupboards. On top of the floor was a water bed—a mattress that could be filled with air or water, to be topped with a featherbed and feather pillows.

Come all you Californians,
    I pray open wide your ears
If you are going across the Plains
    with snotty mules or steers,
Remember beans before you start,
    likewise dried beef and ham,
Beware of ven'son, damn the stuff,
    it's often times a ram.

        —from "Crossing the Plains"

Supplies included a cook stove, water bottles, and food: ham, bacon, fruits, rice, coffee, tea, beans, flour, cornmeal, crackers, butter, and lard. And the ultimate in thinking ahead: Margaret's husband arranged to send lumber for their house around the Horn, since wood was much cheaper in Indiana than in California.

Having more money than most overlanders, Margaret hired a seamstress to "make up a full sup-

Margaret Frink
*Courtesy California
State Library*

ply of clothing, and "packed a trunk full of dress goods not yet made up."

Margaret Frink was quite a curiosity. Riding her own horse, she often was the only woman in her party, prompting wondering remarks like, "There's a lady in the party; and surely there's no man going to take a woman on such a journey as that, across the plains."

Luzena Stanley Wilson was twenty-eight and living in Missouri when she and her husband decided to join the parade to California gold. They spent not much more time preparing for the trek than most of us take to pack for a weekend trip to the beach.

> **It was the work of but a few days to collect our forces for the march into the new country, and we never gave a thought to selling our section, but left it, with two years' labor, for the next comer. Monday we were to be off. Saturday we looked over our belongings, and threw aside what was not absolutely necessary. Beds we must have, and something to eat. It was a strange but comprehensive load which we stowed away in our 'prairie-schooner.'**

And so, within days, Luzena, her husband, and two small children were ready to go.

**Well, on that Monday morning, bright
and early, we were off. With the first
streak of daylight my last cup of
coffee boiled in the wide fire-place,
and the sun was scarcely above the
horizon when we were on the road to
California.**

—Luzena Wilson

**Saying Good-bye Pike County
Farewell for a while,
We'll come back again
When we've panned out our pile!**

—to be sung with courage to the
tune of the chorus of "Oh Susannah"

As they carefully packed treasures to take to the golden land, how could they imagine eventually having to leave these pieces of their lives lying there on the lonely trail? How could they think of things they would wish they had—like more shoes, calico shirts to trade with Indians for food, warm coats for the women and children, and goggles to protect themselves and their draft animals from the dust that ate away at their eyes?

It was only a day's trip for Luzena and her family to the Missouri River, where they ferried across and camped on the other side. They were now in

"Indian Territory." Ahead was a journey across "unbroken, unnamed waste" to California.

Once this thing no longer was simply a parade of the imagination, once they were on their way and actually facing the lonely land forever before them, we can only imagine what they must have been thinking.

What have we done? We must be crazy!

Well, it *was* a crazy thing to do.

> **I little realized then the task I had
> undertaken. If I had, I think I should
> still be in my log cabin in Missouri.
> But when we talked it all over, it
> sounded like such a small task to go
> out to California, and once there
> fortune, of course, would come to us.**
> —Luzena Wilson

On her first morning out, newly-wed forty-niner Catherine Haun woke up with "a strange feeling of fear at the thought of our venturesome undertaking," and "burst into a flood of tears."

But the young honeymooner collected herself.

> **Then wiping away my tears, lest they
> betray me to my husband, I prepared
> to continue my trip. I have often
> thought that had I confided in [my
> husband] he would certainly have
> turned back, for he, as well as the
> other men of the party, was
> disheartened and was struggling not
> to betray it. . . .**

After they "jumped off," how could they know what was ahead? How could they know that for most of those two thousand miles they would walk, because the "trail" was hardly there at all, and the motion of the wagon would toss them around like dolls? How could they know that cholera had followed ships from overseas and now was stalking the forty-niners? How could they know that over the Kansas prairies, the skies could open up and pour rain on them or whirl them around in terrible tornadoes? Or that their men could drown trying to get them across treacherous rivers?

> **Old Noah, he built himself an ark,**
> **There's one more river to cross.**
> **He built it out of hickory bark,**
> **There's one more river to cross.**
> **There's one more river,**
> **And that's the river of Jordan.**
> **There's one more river,**
> **Just one more river to cross.**
>
> —"One More River to Cross,"
> popular camp song

The lazy, wide South Platte River was the first major river crossing. It looked deceptively calm. Luzena described their harrowing but safe crossing, only to look back in horror at the oxen pulling the wagon behind them—sinking slowly into quick sand.

> **They went out of sight inch by inch,**
> **and the water rose over the moaning**
> **beasts. Without a struggle they**
> **disappeared beneath the surface. In a**
> **little while the broad South Platte**
> **swept on its way, sunny, sparkling,**
> **placid, without a ripple to mark**
> **where a lonely man parted with all**
> **his fortune.**

When Margaret Frink joined the parade in 1850, she was aghast at how many others had the same idea.

> It was a grand spectacle when we came, for the first time, in view of the vast emigration, slowly winding its way westward over the broad plain. The country was so level that we could see the long trains of white-topped wagons for many miles. . . . It seemed to me that I had never seen so many human beings in all my life before. . . . And . . . I thought, in my excitement, that if one-tenth of these teams and these people got ahead of us, there would be nothing left for us in California worth picking up. . . . There would only be a few barrels of gold left for us when we got to California.

How could they imagine the deadening monotony of days on days of plodding ever westward, with nothing to look at but the wagon ahead and endless dust and prairie? Or that out of the nothingness could suddenly thunder upon them a mad, dashing stampede of buffalo, carrying along their own animals?

They would pass landmarks both majestic and grotesque, such as Chimney Rock, Scotts Bluff, and Independence Rock, in present-day Wyoming. And they'd better be at Independence Rock by Independence Day, or they could run into winter storms in the mountains. They would dance on the prairie and sing songs of hope and of home to celebrate.

Saddle Rock, Scotts Bluffs (as it was known to the emigrants)
Scotts Bluff National Monument, NE

At South Pass, they would marvel at the ease of passing over the Continental Divide, and then seeing water flowing toward the Pacific Ocean. Here, they might part ways with those bound for Oregon, or maybe decide to go to Oregon themselves. Either way, they would trudge through deserts of dust laced with white alkali (a saline powder). They would feel it attack their eyes, and watch it wear down the animal's hooves.

With misleading maps, or none at all, they would learn of a new cutoff—an easier path, a faster way to get there. Some, desperate to end their misery, would take a new way. And most would pay in added anguish.

And then—just when they couldn't imagine anything worse, it would get worse. They would find themselves in the Forty Mile Desert, a ghostly, ghastly place that smelled of death, in a land littered with oxen and wagon carcasses and aban-

East Face, Sierra Nevada, CA

doned belongings. And no water. If they made it through that God-forsaken desert, then they still faced tall, jagged, snowy mountains to cross.

The amazing thing is that most of them made it.

Nearing the Mother Lode, Margaret Frink noticed one of the few women on the trail:

> **Among the crowds on foot, a negro woman came tramping along through the heat and dust, carrying a cast-iron bake oven on her head, with her provisions and blanket piled on top— all she possessed in the world— bravely pushing on for California.**

Margaret didn't note what the woman wore, but we can imagine that her raggedy clothes were much like everyone else's at that point.

Many women planned their trail clothing optimistically. Catherine Haun paid special attention to the clothes she packed for her "romantic wedding tour." Her trousseau trunk contained underclothing; blue gingham dresses; several aprons, including a light colored one for Sundays, and two bonnets.

Catherine also packed a white cotton dress; a black silk manteaux (cloak), trimmed in velvet and fringe; and a fancy lace bonnet wreathed in tiny pink rosebuds.

With this marvelous costume I had hoped to 'astonish the natives' when I should make my first appearance upon the golden streets of the mining town in which we might locate. Should our dreams of great wealth, acquired over night come true it might be embarrassing not to be prepared with a suitable wardrobe for the wife of a very rich man!

Looking ahead in her diary, I couldn't tell if Catherine Haun made it to California with her "marvelous costume" or not. She wrote of lightening their load before crossing the first mountain, and again in the Black Hills of Wyoming, where they buried barrels of alcohol. Since alcohol was one of the last things to go, I assume that Catherine Haun's "trunk of wearing apparel" never made it.

For most of the trip, Catherine wore a dark woolen dress, which protected her from sun and wind and concealed dust and grime.

> **Never without an apron and a three-cornered kerchief, . . . I presented a comfortable, neat appearance.**

Aprons were important. Some women even ironed their aprons on the trail—until they had to leave their irons behind to lighten the load. After trudging through knee-deep dust, a clean white apron over a filthy dress at the end of the day would lift her spirits and remind her of the home she left behind.

No one could have dreamed up more impractical costumes than those of the emigrant women. Indian women in their practical bark or animal skin clothing must have gaped in wonder at these strange women dragging their torn-up, filthy skirts through the mud and dust and over mountains. The skirts could sweep over a campfire and burst into flames, or get caught under a wagon wheel. Yet the women wore their skirts simply because it was expected. But full skirts had one advantage. With their long, ragged skirts, women could form "shields of modesty" for others to hide behind for emergency stops along the trail.

"I wear bloomers," wrote Lucy Cooke in 1852, "as do most of the women folks in the different companies."

Bloomers bloomed briefly on the California Trail in 1852—after Amelia Bloomer popularized the costume in 1851, and before the rage of public opinion came crashing down on bloomer wearers. Soon, though, most women would feel like the one who said she was brave enough to travel the trail, but not brave enough to wear bloomers.

Women carried with them a certain vanity, and the conviction that they still must strive to look like ladies. And that meant light-skinned. Asked if she wasn't "afraid of being burned black by the sun and wind on the plains," Margaret Frink replied, "Oh, no; and if I am, I can stay in the house until I am bleached out again!"

Milk and butter were luxuries on the trail if the travelers had the foresight to bring along a cow. Catherine Haun wrote of two "milch" cows that followed a wagon belonging to four bachelors. Mothers were especially grateful for the milk, which the cows gave

> all the way to the sink of the
> Humboldt where they died I
> remember the evenings' milking was
> used for supper, but that milked in
> the morning was put into a high tin
> churn and the constant jostling that it
> got all day formed butter and
> delicious butter-milk by night. We all
> were glad to swap some of our food
> for a portion of these delicacies.

Cooking on the trail required creativity, stamina, patience—and often a sense of humor.

> The boys amused themselves killing
> prairie squirrels as they were pleased
> to call them. . . . I am firm in the
> belief that they are *rats*. . . . I
> protested against cooking rats, but

fresh meat has been so scarce and the boys were so sure they were squirrels that they had to be cooked. The pronounced opinion was that they looked too much like rats and tasted too much like fish to ever become very popular as an article of diet.

—Helen Carpenter, 1857

Luzena Wilson's biggest fear in the beginning was Indians. She had read and heard many tales of horrendous deeds, but soon discovered that they were "friendly, of course."

Emigrants were understandably terrified of Indians because of the sensational image created by novelists, newspapermen, and politicians—much like the Indians of 1950s "westerns." Yet many travelers, especially children, developed a fascination and affection for them. Like Luzena, they learned that Indian people were of much more help than harm and, indeed, gave or traded food, moccasins, and other desperately needed items.

Women often were the traders. Margaret Frink wrote of a "squaw's" pleasure to see her, the "white squaw." Margaret traded needles and thread, small mirrors and other trinkets for fish, buffalo, deer, and antelope meat.

As they came closer to California, the invaders marched through land occupied by Paiutes and other tribes whom the emigrants called "Digger" Indians. By the time the gold seekers streamed into their lands, the Indians were themselves terrified and aggressive. By then they were learning all too well of the emigrants' diseases and contempt.

The invaders carried with them their absolute convictions of their own moral and racial superiority. And the farther west they got, the harder they felt toward the Indians they encountered.

Helen Carpenter became exasperated trying to barter with some Indians, speaking first English and then French. "Those stupid Indians did not understand French any better than they did English," she huffed.

The Indians picked up emigrant words, which "excelled in profanity," as one writer put it. He told of a traveler who asked an Indian man where he could find a good place to camp. The Indian assured him that there was "plenty of grass ahead for the 'whoa haws,' but no water for the 'G_d d__ns.'"[5]

Luzena Wilson's fear of Indians led her to ask protection from a company of single men, the Independence Company, "with five mule-teams, good wagons, banners flying, and a brass band playing." The men refused because they "didn't want to be troubled with women and children."

"I am only a woman," Luzena shot back, "but I am going to California, too, and without the help of the Independence Co.!"

Luzena realized that her perspective was changing when "the most unnatural events" became "usual." She noted the cavalier way in which a dead man in a neighboring company was quickly buried before his comrades moved on. "There was no time then to wait, no time to mourn over friend or kindred, no time for anything but the ceaseless march for gold."

When the oxen began to slow down under the weight of their load, Luzena Wilson's husband informed her they'd have to lighten the load. After looking things over, they threw out some bacon and a "very dirty calico apron." Later, Luzena retrieved the bacon, which she fried, using the grease to fill her lard can, and the apron, which she washed with Indian soap-root growing around camp.

> **The next day the teams, refreshed by a whole day's rest and good grazing, seemed as well as ever, and my husband told me several times what a 'good thing it was we left those things; that the oxen seemed to travel as well again.'**
>
> **Long after we laughed over the remembrance of that day, and his belief that the absence of the three pieces of bacon and the dirty apron could work such a change.**

After a "long tramp" of three months, Luzena's company entered the desert.

On the "alkali plain," buzzards and coyotes hovered over a surrealistic scene, the hot earth scorching their feet, dust burning their eyes and parching their tongues. Dead oxen and the bleached bones of men and their abandoned wagons lined the trail.

There in the desert, they once again encountered what remained of the Independence Company, the ones who earlier had snubbed Luzena. Only two men were left. Their comrades had died or headed back home, their mules were dead, and the men were dying of hunger and thirst. Imagine their sur-

Mariposa County History Center, Mariposa, CA

prise and gratitude when Luzena brought them food
and water. "They called me an angel; they showered
blessing on me . . . ," and even came to visit her
years later to recall her kindness there in that death-
surrounded desert.

Margaret Frink told of a miracle in the middle of
what she called the Great Desert. A woman named
Mrs. Foshee was making her way through the desert
with some young men. Their food was gone, and the
men were close to giving up. But Mrs. Foshee kept
urging them "not to despair, to still put their trust in
God, for she was sure they would be provided for."

Just a bit farther, one of the young men came
across a cow tied to some willows. Fastened to her
horns was a note that said the cow couldn't travel
any more, and that anyone in need could kill her for
food. Which they did. The next day, they found a
sack of flour with another note inviting the finder to
use it. Margaret Frink didn't say if both notes were
written in the same Providential handwriting.

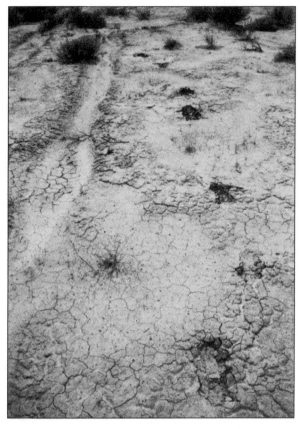

The alkali is a bit like crusted snow. With each step I break through. The wind blows and the earth is hot beneath my feet. By the time they got here, many emigrants had no shoes.
—*from the author's journal.*

From then on, the young men went out of their way to assure Mrs. Foshee's safe passage the rest of the way, and one of them became a minister after he reached California.

> **Praise God from whom**
> **all blessings flow,**
> **Praise Him all creatures here below;**
> **Praise Him above, ye heavenly host,**
> **Praise Father, Son and Holy Ghost.**
>   —"Old One-Hundred"

The parade of marchers that began so buoyantly two thousand miles and more to the east looks a lot different as they straggle into the Mother Lode. But what propelled them to begin sustains them now: GOLD.

> One only hope sustains all these
> unhappy pilgrims, that they will be
> able to get into California alive,
> where they can take a rest, and
> where the gold which they feel sure
> of finding will repay them for all
> their hardships and suffering.
>
> —Margaret Frink

By now the "unhappy pilgrims" form a silent, grotesque procession.

> The emigrants are a woe-begone,
> sorry-looking crowd. The men, with
> long hair and matted beards, in
> soiled and ragged clothes, covered
> with alkali dust, have a half-savage
> appearance. There are but few
> women; among these thousands of
> men, we have not seen more than ten
> or twelve.
>
> —Margaret Frink

It is now five months since they left home. Margaret goes on to describe the "great, splendid trains of fifteen, twenty, or thirty wagons . . . shrunk to three, four, or at most half a dozen" wagon beds with rickety wheels held together with rags drawn by half-dead horses, cattle, and mules with worn-out hooves. Their owners "now trudge along on foot, packing on their backs the scant provisions left. . . ."

As Luzena Wilson neared the end of her journey,

she met a man who had ridden on ahead and was returning to meet his train with a fresh horse and new clothes. Luzena's "womanly vanity" overcame her, and she shrank back in embarrassment at her shabby appearance.

> **My skirts were worn off in rags above my ankles; my sleeves hung in tatters above my elbows; my hands brown and hard, were gloveless; around my neck was tied a cotton square, torn from a discarded dress; the soles of my leather shoes had long ago parted company with the uppers; and my husband and children and all the camp, were habited like myself, in rags.**
>
> **A day or two before, this man was one of us; today, he was a messenger from another world, and a stranger, so much influence does clothing have on our feelings and intercourse with our fellow men.**

Men regularly formed "relief committees" to rescue emigrants as they struggled to safety at the end of their journey. A man who called himself "Mountaineer" wrote to the San Joaquin *Republican* from the relief camp in Sonora in 1853:

> **The emigration . . . is much larger than was expected, and most of them are making longer time than they calculated upon; consequently many of the teams are running short of provisions. . . . There are large numbers of women with the trains,**

> and as Dow jr. says, 'it is enough to
> start tears from the eyes of a baked
> potatoe as to see a white woman
> walking bare foot with a child in her
> arms.' There have been several births
> upon the road, two, at least, here in
> the Sierra Nevada.

Not all incoming gold pilgrims were woe-begone and sorry-looking. Mrs. D.B. Bates marveled at one grand entrance that caused quite a stir in Marysville.

> Two emigrant wagons passed through
> town one day, each driven by two
> beautiful-looking girls—beautiful,
> although browned by exposure to the
> weather. In their hands they carried
> one of those tremendous, long ox-
> whips, which, by great exertion, they
> flourished, to the evident admiration
> of all beholders. Their surpassing
> beauty gained for them the appelation
> of the 'belles of the plains.'

Mrs. Bates reported that the 'belles' were married within two weeks of their arrival.

Lucy Cooke had stayed in Salt Lake with her husband and child for the winter while her father had gone on ahead to California to prepare a home. Nearing the end of the journey, she received a message that there was no home waiting for her. Her father had taken off for the gold rush in Australia!

Orginal Hangtown in 1849.
Now Placerville

Hangtown, 1849 (Placerville)
Courtesy El Dorado County Museum, Placerville, CA

Judge of our disappointment to find, instead of having a good home and friends to go to in San Francisco, we were destitute of either, and with but little means.

After crossing the Sierra Nevada, Lucy and her husband were offered horseback rides into Hangtown. Having had a chance to clean up and change clothes, she planned to make an impression, riding grandly into town wearing her "black brocaded silk frock."

Picture Lucy riding gaily into Hangtown, her horse a trifle ahead of the others. Suddenly the horse went down, rolled over, and deposited Lucy on the sidewalk right in front of a dry goods store, ruining her silk dress. She had indeed made an impression.

Arriving safely in the Mother Lode was something to celebrate. The "Mountaineer" wrote of a dance a few nights after his crew brought emigrants into Sonora:

A few nights since they had a ball at Relief camp, sixteen ladies upon the floor, (excuse me) ground, at the same time, and a lively time they had of it. What was lacking in toilet they made up in good nature.

Many years later, as Lucy Cooke lay dying, she must have been dreaming of her long-ago journey across the plains to the land of gold. "Aren't we almost there?" she asked. "It seems such a long, long way."

CHAPTER FOUR

Luzena Wilson and the Coming of the Carnival Frontier[1]

**'Twas the song of a dream
and the dream of a singer,
Drawn fine in its delicate
fibres of gold . . .**

—from "Isles of the Amazons"
by Joaquin Miller

This part of the parade has arrived. It is quieter now than when it left two thousand miles ago by land, many more thousands by sea. The clowns no longer are laughing. The tricksters have gone Some Place Else, or disappeared into the crowd. Some have changed their masks.

As the massive parade by land and sea continued to pour into the Mother Lode and its gateways, it would become what some have called a carnival— a gaudy, multicolored world of wild surprise, spinning madly from comedy to tragedy, from rich to poor, from kindness to cruelty, and back again.

Out there on the desert, or in the doldrums, the tempo had slowed to a death march. But the dream kept them going and pulled them across the menacing mountain or sinister sea and delivered them— most of them—to the land of gold. The dream is just as clear now as when they joined the parade.

Nearing the end of her journey, a ragged Luzena

Wilson wearily began to cook yet one more meal over a campfire. She had come close to death out there on the trail. Now, as she straggled the last miles with her husband and two little children, she wondered how they would get food and money.

As if in answer, a miner, seeing a rare sight—a woman—approached her.

"I'll give you five dollars, ma'am, for them biscuit," he said, and then offered double that amount. He reached out and placed a shining gold piece in her hand. I picture her, brushing her stringy hair from her face, staring at this small, magical thing that has lured her and thousands of others to this place. Here, shining in her hand, was her future. Clenching the dream, Luzena Wilson clinched her first deal as a gold rush entrepreneur.

In my dreams that night I saw crowds of bearded miners striking gold from the earth with every blow of the pick, each one seeming to leave a share for me.

When she awoke the next day, Luzena looked for her treasure. It was gone. It was an omen—the first of many fortunes she would make and lose as quickly as the spin of the wheel of fortune in the land of gold.

"The nest egg was gone," she concluded, "but the homely bird which laid it—the power and will to work—was still there." It was a conviction she would draw from many times in the coming months and years.

Soon she was at journey's end on the edge of Sacramento, a river town crammed with miners and merchants mining the miners. This was where Johann Sutter had begun to build his now-crumbling empire.

Luzena and her family still weren't in the gold country. To get there they would have to go back into the Sierra foothills to the east and north. But Luzena's family needed food and a place to live. Now. That would require some money, and they didn't have any.

She looked around and couldn't see one other woman. In her six months living in Sacramento, she saw only two women. Luzena would soon learn one of the advantages of being a lone woman among men. She walked into a bank—about the only real building in a canvas town—and boldly asked for a loan. Imagine her surprise when she walked out with one. There were no loans for men, but the bank would float a loan for a woman.

With some of her borrowed money, Luzena bought food for her family. Back at her home-tent, she tossed some salt pork into a hot pan, and watched in fascination as "it pranced, it sizzled, frothed over the pan, sputtered, crackled, and acted as if possessed. . . . and my pork had vanished into smoke." Another omen. Luzena Wilson's first fortune would vanish nearly as quickly.

They needed more money, and there was only one place to get it—sell the oxen, those gentle beasts that had brought them two thousand miles to this place. With the six hundred dollars, Luzena and her husband (who remained nameless through her entire narrative) bought an interest in a hotel and began to take in boarders.

As Luzena entered the hotel's living room—the first room she'd been in since she left home back in Missouri, she entered a world that would become a metaphor for scenes she would encounter in her gold country travels.

Peering through the murky light, she saw what appeared to be a scene of calm and camaraderie. Candles stuck in whiskey bottles dimly danced on the faces of the men drinking at the bar. Taking orders was the barkeep dressed in "half sailor, half vaquero fashion." A handful of men danced to the tune of "Moneymusk," played on a cracked fiddle. Along one wall, men lay on bunks stacked from floor to ceiling. One young man was tearfully reading a letter from home, and others lay sleeping. Some were sick. Then she saw it.

> **Out from another bunk, upon this curious mingling of merriment and sadness stared the white face of a corpse. They had forgotten even to cover the still features with the edge of a blanket, and he lay there, in his rigid calmness, a silent unheeded witness to the acquired insensibility**

**of the early settlers. What was one
dead man, more or less! Nobody
missed him. The music and the
dancing, the card-playing, drinking,
and swearing went on unchecked by
the hideous presence of Death. His
face grew too familiar in those days
to be a terror.**

Luzena must have remembered that feeling of
dread she had felt out there on the desert, when she
saw the indifference to others' suffering when people's own survival was at stake. It was one of the
biggest fears women had—losing their humanity.

Now here it was right in front of her, and she
acknowledged with shame that in her own rush to
work and make money, she "grew hard-hearted like
the rest." It must have made her heart sick to
remember that time she was too busy to heed the
moans coming from the canvas house right next to
hers. Then one day the sounds stopped. When she
looked in, she saw a sight she would never forget. A
young man lay there—dead, "with not even a
friendly hand to close his eyes." She didn't even
know who he was.

How would his family know what happened to
him? Her thoughts flew to her own young sons, and
to the dead man's mother.

**Many a time since . . . have I wept
for the sore heart of that poor boy's
mother, and I have prayed that if
ever want and sickness came to mine,
some other woman would be more
tender than I had been, and give
them at least a glass of cold water.**

For Luzena's own family, life went on, and within two months she and her husband sold their investment for a thousand dollars in gold dust. Real gold dust! Did it glow as brightly as that first gold she held in her hand and then lost? It didn't glow in their possession for long, because they traded it for a commodity they were sure to profit from: barley.

"The population of Sacramento was largely a floating one," Luzena noted. "Today there might be ten thousand people in the town, and tomorrow four thousand of them might be on their way to the gold fields."

Soon, Sacramento's population really was floating—in a fierce flood that would carry away most of their home, along with their barley. Destitute once more, the little family took refuge on the second floor of the hotel they had just sold, where the water "splashed upon the ceiling" below.

Luzena's description of that eerie night can not be matched for its poetry and meaning.

Sometimes for a moment the light shone through, but only long enough to make the darkness blacker. And the waters rushed and roared, and pale, set faces peered into the darkness, upon the hurrying monster which swallowed up in its raging fury the results of their hard labors and their perseverance.

For seventeen days Luzena and her family waited, along with one other family, and perhaps thirty-
five men. For seventeen days they listened to the
wind and water assaulting the frame building, feeling its shudders. From the rushing waters, they
caught sacks of onions and other soggy food to eat,
carefully avoiding the rats perched on the floating
debris.

**There were few close ties and few
friendships; and when a familiar face
dropped out no one knew whether the
man was dead or gone away; nobody
inquired, nobody cared. The
character of the pioneers was a
paradox. They were generous to a
degree which we can scarcely realize,
yet selfish beyond parallel.**

Finally, the waters retreated, and Luzena's husband rebuilt their canvas house using the wooden
supports left from the first one. Worried about
another flood, Luzena's husband devised a "floating
floor, which rose and sank with the tide." When
Luzena would wake up in the night, she'd reach
down and touch the water, and if it didn't reach a
certain notch on the bed post, she'd go back to
sleep. If the water was higher, they would prepare
to evacuate.

Their fortune gone, all around them was ruin.
"The canvas city was laid low; the wooden houses
stood like grim sentinels in the waste, and slime
and drift-wood covered the whole town."

Luzena knew there had to be Some Place Else—
some place safe from having their dreams, and
maybe their lives, washed away. And so, they decided to follow rumors of a gold strike at the tent camp

called Deer Creek Diggins (now Nevada City), in the
northern Mother Lode country.

The family hitched a ride with a man who offered
horseback transportation and a wagon with oxen, all
on credit. For twelve wrenching days, they climbed
and slogged through seas of mud and over steep
mountains. At one point in the journey, where "the
whole surface of the mountain side was a smooth,
slippery rock, the oxen stiffened out their legs, and
wagon and all literally slid down a quarter of a
mile." It could have been a hilarious scene, but the
weary little band probably was too tired to laugh.

When at last they inched over the last mountain,
Luzena looked down on "a row of canvas tents lining each of the two ravines."

> **Great, brawny miners wielded the
> pick and shovel, while others stood
> knee deep in the icy water, and
> washed the soil from the gold. Every
> one seemed impelled by the frenzy of
> fever as men hurried here and there,
> so intent upon their work they had
> scarcely time to breathe.**

Luzena's entrance into the town of tents and
brush huts was not a "triumphal" one. She fervent-
ly wished for a "back way" to come in; the whole
procession was mud from head to foot.

> **I remember filling my wash-basin
> three times with fresh water before I
> had made the slightest change
> apparent in the color of my face; and
> I am sure I scrubbed till my arms
> ached, before I got the children back
> to their natural hue.**

Luzena was among hundreds who would stream into Deer Creek Diggins after word got out about the gold. James Marshall had discovered some gold here in the summer of 1848, but true to the luck of this hard-luck man, he failed to see the possibilities, and moved on. A few miners struck it rich later that summer. One of them was a Madam Penn, who worked beside her husband carrying dirt and working their rocker. Luzena never mentioned Madam Penn—perhaps because she didn't consider Madam Penn a lady, and therefore not memorable.

The Wilsons found a space in camp for their new home and built it that very day. But it wasn't made of canvas. Since there was no money, this house would have to be free.

> **We were not rich enough to indulge in the luxury of a canvas home; so a few pine boughs and branches of the undergrowth were cut and thrown into a rude shelter for the present, and my husband hurried away up the mountain to begin to split out 'shakes' for a house.**

Luzena laid their bedding inside their brush house and set up her cook stove under the shade of a pine tree. She was home.

Now at this point, most of us would stretch out for a snooze. Not Luzena. While her husband was away for the afternoon, she went to work. With her own hands, she "chopped stakes, drove them into the ground," and set up a table. Her husband returned to find twenty paying customers for dinner al fresco, each paying a dollar in gold.

Luzena was in business. She felt like a queen among all those men. In her presence, the "motley

crowd" would lower their voices and stop swearing and arguing. And even more amazing than that, some miners actually came forty miles over mountains, "just to look at me, and I never was called a handsome woman, in my best days, even by my most ardent admirers."

Luzena happened to be at that place for that brief moment in Mother Lode history right after a gold discovery when the world seemed to pause before the coming chaos.

> **The world will never see the like again of those 'pioneers of '49'. They were, as a rule, upright, energetic, and hard-working, many of them men of education and culture whom the misfortune of poverty had forced into the ranks of labor in this strange country. The rough days which earned for California its name for recklessness had not begun. There was no shooting, little gambling, and less theft in those first months. The necessities of hard work left no leisure for the indulgence even of one's temper, and the 'rough' element**

**which comes to every mining country
with the first flush times had not yet
begun to crowd the West.**

As "flush times" began to crowd this country, Deer Creek Diggins became Nevada—Spanish for snowy. After the state stole Nevada's name, the town became Nevada City.

As the surface gold got scarcer, the miners teamed up to work the rockers, long toms, and sluice boxes—all bigger tools based on the idea of separating the heavier gold from the dirt, gravel, or sand. Some of the miners dug straight down into the hillsides, bringing up earth to wash. They called the shafts "coyote" mines because they resembled coyote burrows. The men rigged up windlasses to lower buckets into the shafts to bring the dirt and gravel to the surface to be washed.

Most of the coyotes were in "dry diggins"—not close to water. So the miners had either to haul the dirt to water, or bring the water to the dirt by diverting streams or building ditches and flumes. As the water flowed, the gold flowed into the miners' pockets.

"The 'Coyote Diggings' . . . were very rich in coarse gold, and money came pouring into the town." Luzena by now was doing fine, thank you. She did so well that her husband joined her in the enterprise. She paid off the debt to the man who had brought them, and expanded the business, serving up to two hundred boarders at twenty-five dollars a week. She "became luxurious and hired a cook and waiters."

Meanwhile, a carnival parade of ten thousand had marched into Nevada City. "Everybody had money," Luzena remembered, "and everybody spent it. Money ran through one's fingers like water through a sieve."

Leading the parade were the gamblers, who offered a place for the miners to gather and have some company—and part with their money. Lining the streets were drinking and gambling joints. "Possessed of the demon of recklessness," the miners "sang, danced, drank and caroused all night, and worked all day."

Knives and pistols multiplied. Wars between miners and gamblers, miners and Indians, Americans and foreigners brought blood and death. Disease preyed on miners already weakened from constant exposure to cold water and exhausting work.

The gold seemed to pour out of the earth and into Luzena's hands—just as she had dreamed. Consider: if you're gathering gold beyond your imagination, you can't keep it with you all the time, and there's no bank, no safe to put it in. So what do you do with it?

Many of the miners took their gold to Luzena for safekeeping. And so Luzena became both a banker and a lender, charging ten dollars a month interest. She stored her clients' gold under her mattress—and in her oven, just like Molly in the movie *The Unsinkable Molly Brown.* Luzena once missed a bag of gold, and found her little boy playing with it in the street. No one bothered him.

Within six months, Luzena and her husband had twenty thousand dollars worth of property and investments.

Like Molly Brown's gold, Luzena's burned up—along with the whole town when a fire started nearby. Eighteen months after the Wilson family's arrival in Deer Creek Diggins, Nevada City lay in ashes. Luzena's hotel and the money were gone, except for the five hundred dollars her husband happened to have in his pocket the day of the fire.

Once again, Luzena described an ugly disaster in beautiful words.

**The red glare . . . wrapped the
moving human creatures in a fiendish
glow, and cast their giant shadows far
along the ground. The fire howled
and moaned like a giant in an agony
of pain, and the buildings crashed
and fell as if he were striking them
down in his writhings. When the slow
dawn broke, and the sun came riding
up so calm and smiling, he looked
down upon a smouldering bed of
ashes . . ..**

It seemed inevitable. Luzena collapsed. She had worked herself to exhaustion. The fire had taken away everything she had worked for, and her strength along with it. For weeks she lay sick. When she recovered enough to travel, the little family headed once more for Sacramento.

So why didn't they rebuild? Luzena didn't say, but by then Nevada City was not at all the same place as when it was Deer Creek Diggins. Maybe she looked around at the gambling halls and saloons, loud men and wild women, the piles of garbage and mine tailings, and decided it no longer was where she wanted to be. There must be Some Place Else to raise a family.

Soon they were headed back to Sacramento. On the way, Luzena was amazed to discover herself traveling on a real road. The trip that had taken twelve days eighteen months ago now took two.

Once in Sacramento, Luzena couldn't believe what her eyes were telling her. The drowned town they had left now had real sidewalks, and brick and

mortar houses, and theaters. For the first time in
California, Luzena saw walls that were papered and
painted. She also saw gambling houses, bordellos,
and whiskey shops. The "sporting population"
turned out for the bull fights and mustang races.
Desperadoes strutted around daring anyone to get
between them and their gold, whatever form it took.
There was a murder nearly every day, and Luzena
witnessed more than one gruesome lynching.

And then there were the rats. The deserted
Sacramento hotel where Luzena's family lived was
infested with rats—

> **rats that galloped madly over the**
> **floor and made journeys from room**
> **to room through openings they had**
> **gnawed in the panels. They seemed to**
> **have no apprehension of human**
> **beings and came and went as**
> **fearlessly as if we had not been there.**

Luzena described the rats' cavortings in elegant
detail. They danced back and forth on the ropes and
chains of the vessels at the piers, and "in that

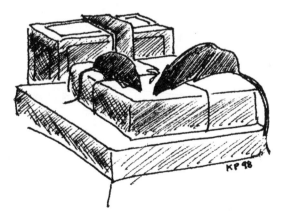

deserted house it seemed that all [of them] had gathered there to hold high carnival." When her husband threw barley on the ground to see how many would come, they covered the yard within minutes—seemingly "piled three deep in their ravenous hunger for the grain."

Maybe the rat carnival was one reason Luzena and her family didn't stay long in Sacramento. But she didn't go home to Missouri. She probably enjoyed her freedom too much to want to return. So the little family picked up their dreams once more and moved on to Some Place Else.

In the two years since she had arrived in the country of the Mother Lode, Luzena Wilson had made and lost several fortunes, and witnessed the arrival of the carnival that was the California Gold Rush.

Luzena and her family moved on to a valley where "the calmness and silence of the wide prairie soothed us like a sweet dream." It was their final Some Place Else, and the Wilsons would be among the founding citizens of the place that would become Vacaville.

There, Luzena once again set up her stove and camp kettle and opened a hotel under a tall oak tree. She made a table with boards from their wagon bed and surrounded it with stumps and logs for chairs. Hotel guests slept on the other side of the haystack, while the family slept under their canvas wagon cover. Though hardly fancy, Luzena's hotel soon "had the reputation of being the best on the route from Sacramento to Benicia."

As the earth turned colder, the Wilsons began to build more permanent shelter, and permanent lives. Like many pioneer women, Luzena exulted in long horseback rides. Saddling up with her husband's saddle, which she boldly rode astride, she secured her boys behind her and explored the countryside and visited her far-flung neighbors. She attended an extravagant Spanish ball, and mingled with the Spanish-speaking landowners until "the Spanish population vanished before the coming immigration."

Luzena's husband raised a fine crop of hay and got it all baled. But "trouble seemed to follow us relentlessly," and rains ruined the hay. The only thing that kept the family financially afloat was Luzena's hotel.

The Wilsons were among the forty-niners who invested in land, and became involved in endless boundary disputes over Spanish land grants. Luzena's husband battled "squatters" and the courts, which kept them "in a state of continuous ferment."

kp 98

But life went on and became more settled. Luzena helped start a school "in a little blue cotton house under a tree" that would become Pacific Methodist College. With no doctor nearby, Luzena became a "general practitioner and apothecary for the neighborhood," and came to think of herself as a "genuine doctor."

"I don't think I ever killed anybody," she noted, "and I am quite sure I cured a good many of my patients."

The Wilsons often hosted town balls in their dining room, and "not seldom the town overflowed for the night with the buxom lads and lassies from thirty miles away."

As a forty-niner, Luzena was one of those driven souls who made it through the grueling journey to the Mother Lode, and saw the awakening of the gold frontier. As a pioneer, she saw the transition from the stagecoaches and "the rollicking, unassuming fun of the country" to the railroads and "the aping of city airs and the following of city fashions." Where ladies once came to country dances "in calico dresses and calf boots," now they attended parties "befrizzled and montagued, with silk dresses, eight-button gloves, and French slippers with Pompadour heels."

Luzena Wilson's quest for gold never brought her lasting wealth. But she made a life for herself in this golden land that probably couldn't have happened anywhere else. She came to a land where a person could take a chance and risk everything, lose it all, and risk again. Where she could build a future with her own hands. Where a woman would have the kind of freedom that would make it all possible.

At a time when most women's worlds were small, Luzena took hers by the tail and flung it to the winds of fortune right in the middle of a carnival. At a time when most women were forced to choose between marriage and making their own lives, Luzena Stanley Wilson did it all.

CHAPTER FIVE

Masks of Comedy and Tragedy

Many an occurrence of those terrible days would have been funny, had we not been so filled with fear, and had not tragedy trodden so closely on the heels of comedy.

—Luzena Wilson

It was a world of mad surprise where you could discover gold right at your feet. You'd be walking along—after a storm, say—and there it would be, staring you in the face.

One story goes that California gold was discovered not by a man but by a woman who was cooking a chicken for an old Indian chief and discovered gold in the fowl's gizzard. Well, we know that Indian people knew about the gold long before the White Faces did. And it could very well have been a woman who discovered it. As for showing up in the chicken gizzard, if it could happen anywhere, it would have happened in California.

There were tales like the one of the preacher praying over the body of a deceased miner beside his open grave. One of the mourners spied something that looked like gold embedded in the freshly-overturned dirt. So before the "Amen," everyone jumped in the hole and started digging for gold, leaving the body out in the cold.

There was the sad story of the old English couple who had worked the mines together and made their pile. They were heading home with their gold dust and didn't want anyone they might meet to know how much they were carrying. Concealing the gold in their belts, they boarded a boat to take them to the steamer that would carry them home. The boat capsized, and the couple, unable to swim with all that gold around their waists, sank and drowned.[1]

Men would be walking down a mud path politely called a street, see something glinty right in front of them, and soon the street would be all torn up.

A woman mined five hundred dollars worth of gold from her kitchen floor.

You'd pull up a shrub that was in your way, and there would be a lump of gold stuck right there in the roots.

As long as there seemed to be enough gold to go around, the miners pretty much minded their own business with their picks and shovels, pans, and rockers. At that point, the ones with the gold should have taken their money and run. But most of them didn't.

Although miners tried to keep their strikes to themselves, word usually got out, and pretty soon ravenous gold seekers would be swarming all over the place. If a claim didn't seem to be panning out, there must be a better one Some Place Else. One miner who went south complained that so many miners were crammed into the northern mines that half the men had to stand up while the other half slept.

As they roamed from camp to camp, nobody cared who they were or where they came from.

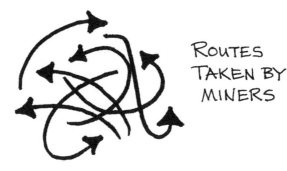

ROUTES
TAKEN BY
MINERS

Oh, what was your name
 in the States?
Was it Thompson or Johnson
 or Bates?
Did you murder your wife
And fly for your life?
Say, what was your name
 in the States?

—traditional miners' ditty

It was a pretty grim life, mining. Most miners couldn't work year round because of snows or constant rain in winter, and not enough water in summer. Many worked in ravines so deep they never saw the light of day. Some would stand knee deep in icy water all day, panning. Others would work sluice boxes, cradles, long toms, and coyotes shoveling tons of soil and gravel every day. Accidents claimed many lives and many men's health.

The hordes of gold hunters coming from every direction brought Asiatic cholera, small pox, malaria, typhoid, typhus, and other infections with them over land and sea. A cholera outbreak in San Francisco in 1850 killed one thousand people, and sent half its population of six thousand fleeing into the countryside.[2] Garbage heaps, open sewers, com-

Mining with the Long Tom
Courtesy California State Library

mon towels and drinking cups—all spread diseases
that traveled as fast as gold fever.

Most miners were too exhausted to cook or pay
attention to their diets. Mostly they lived on bacon,
beans, and pan bread, flap jacks, sour dough bread,
or rock-hard biscuit. Despite efforts by conscien-
tious cooks to serve fruits and vegetables, poor
diets and food shortages caused scurvy, and perhaps ten thousand forty-eighters and forty-niners
died of it.[3]

> I toiled night and day
>   with the hope of gaining wealth,
> Through the cold winter's rain
>   with delight;
> But alas! sad misfortune has ruined
>   my health,
> So my fond friends at home,
>   all, good night.
>   —from "The Miner's Lament"

Elisha Douglass Perkins left his young wife back in Ohio with the dream of striking it rich and proving that he was worthy of her. He arrived in September 1849. The death of a friend from scurvy four months later carried his thoughts home:

> **The death of one of our number here so far away from home & all that makes life dear, casts a gloom on all the survivors & we cannot but think of the possibility of a like fate being reserved for ourselves, & oh how terrible the thought. If I must die, let me but get home & die in the arms of my friends, & I'll not complain, but here with no one to care for me, or shed a tear of affection as my spirit takes its flight, tis horrible. . . . California has been, & will be the cause of many broken hearts & much grief, & I look forward to my release from it with great anxiety.**

Two weeks after the death of his friend, Elisha Perkins wrote of eking out barely enough gold to meet expenses.

> **We hope however when spring opens to be able to commence a more successful life & shall get along as well as our impatience will let us till that time.**

The miners lived in perpetual hope of "things opening up in the spring." But for Elisha, they never did. He never struck it rich, and never went home, too embarrassed to return with empty pockets.

On the other hand, many echoed the feelings of twenty-year-old John Ingalls when he wrote from Hangtown to his foster brother back home:

> **How I wish you could have been here with me this winter. I think you would have enjoyed it first rate.   I NEVER ENJOYED MYSELF BETTER IN MY LIFE.**[4]

John never returned home, and his brother never came to California, but John's young wife did.

One of the few mining town luxuries might be food prepared by a woman, depending on her skills, and what was available. It was hard even to plan a menu, because a cook never knew what might make it to camp. It all depended on where the ships came from with their cargo, and what could be packed into the camps. It truly was pot luck. She might get gulls' eggs from Colombia, dried fruits from Chile, and bananas, cocoanuts, or yams from the Sandwich Islands. Sometimes the flour from New York warehouses would be so vermin infested she'd have to sift out the long black worms before she could use it.

In this "weird and strange" world, Luzena Wilson observed that although the country was overrun with cattle, "fresh milk and butter were unheard of," so she served milk for a dollar a pint. A sick miner would pay a dollar and a half for a bowlful of porridge, made of half water, half milk, and a little flour.

One miner gave his own "receipt" for plum pudding. Recipes, by the way, were "receipts" in those days; "recipe" was too high-fallutin'. And the "plums" for the pudding were raisins.

OLD-FASHIONED PLUM PUDDING
or PLUM DUFF

> Just take some flour, put it into a
> sack, slap in some water, you know;
> throw in some salt, a little spice, a
> hunk of butter, and then some dried
> apples, if there ain't any raisins
> around, then some eggs, and that ends
> the programme. Then shake 'em all
> together a spell, put the sack in the
> kettle and let her bile till 'tis done,
> and you have got something fit to eat,
> or anyway you oughter have if 'tis
> mixed all right.[5]

The miner must not have mixed it right because after he "biled" it for six hours, "the derned thing was so tough that we couldn't cut it with a knife." So he threw it away. Fifteen years later some miners uncovered the plum duff, and all who saw it thought the spotted stone to be of great archeological significance.

This miner could have used some help from someone like Luzena. Once they got to the diggings, many men discovered how much they missed the work that women did—mainly feeding them and cleaning up their messes. Having a woman around was cause for doing a jig! Here was someone to cook and sew and wash their clothes—just like at home.

> **Whoora! for a live woman in the mines. What'll the boys say? They'll peel out o' their skins in the mines! . . . Wheat bread and chicken fixins now—hoe cakes and slapjacks . . . whoora!**[6]

As more miners swarmed into the Mother Lode, the women who did "women's work" toiled even harder, and the food became fancier and more plentiful. In a letter to the son she left behind, Mary Ballou described her work in a boarding house in Negrobar, not far from Sacramento, in October 1852.

A Live Woman in the Mines
Courtesy California State Library

> [S]omtimes I am making mince pie
> and Apple pie and squash pies.
> Somtimes frying mince turnovers and
> Donuts. I make Buiscuit and now and
> then Indian jonny cake and then
> again I am making minute puding
> filled with rasons and Indian Bake
> pudings and then again a nice plum
> Puding and then again I am Stuffing
> a Ham of pork that cost forty cents a
> pound. Somtimes I am . . . making
> gruel for the sick now and then
> cooking oisters sometimes making
> coffee for the French people strong
> enough for any man to walk on that
> has Faith as Peter had. three times a
> day I set my Table which is about
> thirty feet in length and do all the
> little fixings about it such as filling
> pepper boxers and venegar cruits and
> mustard pots and Butter cups.

Boarding houses and hotels in the Mother Lode became famous for extravagant menus. Better roads allowed stage coaches to bring exotic foods from around the world. Luzena Wilson called the stage driver the most important person in town, even above the bartender.

A hot item brought in the stages was oysters— oysters for frying, oysters for pie, oysters to guzzle with champagne. Oysters were a metaphor for the carnival frontier. They showed up at the most elegant and expensive hotel, and in the most humble mining camp.

Californians' demand for oysters was so prodigious that the beds of San Francisco Bay were nearly gone by 1851, sending oystermen north to hunt new beds. Oysterville, Washington was founded to supply the mollusks for California.

One of the most famous Mother Lode inventions was Hangtown Fry, first cooked up at the Cary House Hotel in Hangtown. It seems a miner, loaded with gold dust and probably liquor, sauntered up to the counter and demanded the most expensive dish in the house. Eggs (one dollar each) and fresh oysters (six dollars each) happened to be the most expensive ingredients, so the chef made up a receipt, throwing in some bacon at the miner's request.

HANGTOWN FRY[7]

1/2 pound bacon
6–10 oysters, preferably Olympia
        (Washington) oysters,
        the smaller the better
1 egg beaten with a teaspoon of milk
soda cracker crumbs
6 eggs
1/4 cup milk or cream
1/4 cup each chopped parsley
        and fresh grated
        Parmesan cheese (optional)
    Fry the bacon until almost crisp
and set aside. Pat the oysters dry and
dip them in the beaten egg ("run it
through an egg wash" in
Restaurantese) and then coat them
with the cracker crumbs. Saute in
cooking oil until almost cooked.
    In a mixing bowl, beat 6 eggs with

Cary House Hotel, Placerville (Hangtown), CA home of Hangtown Fry.
Courtesy El Dorado County Museum, Placerville, CA

milk or cream, parsley and grated cheese if desired, and salt and pepper to taste. Pour the egg mixture over the oysters in the pan, reduce heat to low, and scramble the eggs, lifting them with a spatula when they're nearly done to let the uncooked eggs run underneath. When the eggs are set, place the pan under a broiler to brown lightly. Transfer to a heated platter and garnish with crumbled bacon and parsley. Serves six.

Hangtown got its name from the hangings of several robbers in 1849. Of course there were many hangtowns, but this was the place where the name stuck. Civic-minded residents later changed the name to the more acceptable Placerville.

Having someone to do the wash was almost as much of a relief as having a cook. Some say that miners got so desperate for someone else to wash their filthy duds that they actually sent them to the Sandwich Islands or even to China for laundering.

KP 98

Figuring in the time that would take stretches the imagination. It's more likely that the desperate ones would wear their trademark red or blue shirts and canvas pants until they were ready to fall off, and then just throw them out the window. There the foul rags would enrich the content of the pervasive mud, along with the potato peelings, bones, boots, pots and pans, egg shells, cabbage leaves, whiskey bottles, oyster tins, and stove-pipe hats and fancy shoes brought by Yankee miners.

Pure mud was bad enough, but mining camp mud was downright repulsive. Mrs. Lee Whipple-Haslam remembered the day Irish Kate, a laundress, was walking a narrow trail, carrying clean laundry, and fell into ten feet of "slum" (mud filled with mining refuse). "It required half a dozen men with ropes to land her on terra firma."

Strangely, Luzena Wilson never mentioned any critters she had to contend with other than rats. But there were plenty of pesky and dangerous varmints, in addition to rats and gamblers. Grizzlies, mountain lions, and black bear prowled around, occasionally strolling into a cabin looking for a handout. Mary Ballou routinely chased hogs out of her kitchen and mules from her dining room, along with an occasional rat from her bedroom.

Abby Mansur, living in Horseshoe Bar in 1852, wailed to her sister in a letter about the fleas that would surely send her to hell by making her swear.

> **you cannot take any comfort for the
> fleas if you sit down to rest or go to
> bed there is no comfort for you the
> flease are biting or the bedbugs or
> both and you might Just as well be in
> hell   i never swore so much in my
> life   i always swore bad enough but
> if i should die now god only knows
> that would become of me . . .
> sometimes i have to get up a half
> dozen times in the night to hunt
> flease and besides bear the
> punishment they inflict on me   i am
> sore the whole time from the effects
> of there bites**

When Luzena Wilson recorded her life as a forty-niner, she did it from a distance, thirty years after the Gold Rush, and she left some things out. Not once, for example, did she mention the Indian people in Nevada City. Did she not know of the battles going on between miners and Indians in 1850 very close to Nevada City or of the attempted treaty that was never ratified by the government? Was she not

The Arnett family, Washo
Suzie and her husband, and her mother, Sally
Courtesy Calaveras County Historical Society, San Andreas, CA

aware that the Indian people whose land her people had invaded were dying by the thousands from miners' diseases and violence?

Nor did Luzena refer to the many homelands of the miners who came with the carnival parade.

One observer neatly categorized the nationalities of the seekers who came to the Mother Lode:

> **Australia sent criminals, Italy musicians, Germany barbers and beer drinkers, England pugilists, France bullies and prostitutes, Mexico monte players, Chile sneak thieves and pick pockets, Peru malefactors, Ireland highway robbers, and the United States politicians and plotters and also, now and then, a man of propriety with his following of artisans and farmers.[8]**

Among Nevada City's population by 1851 were Chinese, Spanish speakers, Blacks, French, Irish, and Germans. An illustrious visitor in 1851 was none other than the German adventurer Heinrich Schliemann, who would go on to discover and plunder the mythical city of Troy. Schliemann found Nevada City "a small and extremely nasty place in the midst of a pine-forest."[9]

Among all these nationalities were women. Those not classified as "ladies" are hard to track during the Gold Rush. The "real" ladies were light-skinned English speakers, generally North American. It helped to be Protestant and Yankee (not a "Missourian" or Catholic). Proper ladylike dress and behavior, even in the mining camps, was expected.

In journals, reminiscences, and letters, "ladies" politely tried to avoid mentioning prostitutes. And miners were, of course, careful not to reveal too much knowledge of unladylike ladies. And so, women from other countries, and certainly Indian women, are missing from many gold rush writings and official records.

Louise Clappe became famous for her letters to her sister back East describing her life in the mining camp of Rich Bar, far to the north of Nevada City. "Dame Shirley," which became her pen name, was a forty-niner who sailed around the Horn with her doctor husband. In her letters, she described a panorama of colorful women in the carnival parade passing before her eyes.

Riding a mule to Rich Bar, Dame Shirley encountered Indian women. Seeing them through the lenses of her own culture, she described them as "degraded wretches," "poor creatures," and "wildwood Cleopatras." She later described their lifeways with better understanding and sympathy.

The "Indiana Girl" was a "gigantic piece of humanity" with a "mighty voice," who wore miners' boots and "has the dainty habit of wiping her dishes on her apron." She had walked to the Rich Bar the previous spring, packing fifty pounds of flour on her back through five feet of snow.

One woman tended bar at the boarding house she ran with her husband. Another, according to an admiring male observer, "earnt her old man . . . nine hundred dollars in nine weeks, clear of all expenses, by washing!" A "little Kanaka" (Hawaiian) woman worried that Dame Shirley was serious when she jokingly told the mother she wanted her baby.

There was the "long woman," whose husband had died of cholera a few weeks into the journey. Here in Rich Bar, she was living under a large tree and sleeping in her covered wagon with her ten children, including a nursing infant. She took in washing, and the miners paid more than she asked. "She made me think of a long-legged, very thin hen, scratching for dear life, to feed her never-to-be-satisfied brood."

In the dawning of the mining frontier, the Sabbath generally was honored as a day of rest. With the arrival of Carnival, the miners still took the Sabbath off, but they turned it into a day of revelry. In 1852, Dame Shirley wrote:

**The Sabbath in California is kept,
when kept at all, as a day of hilarity
and baccanalian sports, rather than
as a season of holy meditation or
religious devotion. Horseracing, cock-
fighting, cony-hunting, card-playing,
theatrical performances, and other
elegant amusements are freely
engaged in on this day.**

Dame Shirley forgot to mention fighting in the above description. In one "customary" Sabbath day fight involving North Americans and "Spaniards," an American was fatally stabbed. Like so many Keystone Kops, the Hispanics and the Americans started chasing one another around the camp.

Finally the Americans settled down long enough to elect a Vigilance Committee, who immediately selected their culprit: a Spanish-speaking woman who packed a pair of pistols, and had always worn pants. The charges against her were unclear, though the feeling was that "she was the *indirect* cause of the fight." Dame Shirley concluded, "You see always, it is the old, cowardly excuse of Adam in Paradise: 'The woman tempted me, and I did eat.'"

The committee sentenced the woman to leave town. Which she did.

The well-known "respect" for women in the West often falls apart for women like her. It may not have mattered where a man came from, but a woman's past mattered, and so did her appearance. A woman "deserving" respect was one who appeared to be a "lady." A dark-skinned woman who wore pants and packed pistols broke the rules and therefore was no "lady," so the rule of respect didn't apply to her.

In 1851, a woman in Downieville broke the rules

and paid with her life. She was a "dark señorita"—
a dangerous thing to be. Details are hazy, and vary
with different accounts. It happened the day after
July 4, the Mother Lode's most notorious holiday, a
day of high carnival.

A huge Scottish miner broke into a cabin where
Juanita (some call her Josepha) lived with her husband (some say lover). The Scot left but returned
the next day. His friends said he came to apologize.
Juanita said he threatened her and called her a
whore. She stabbed him and he died.

A mob gathered, swarming like hornets. A hasti-
ly appointed "jury" pronounced Juanita guilty of
murder and sentenced her to hang. Before anyone
had a chance to think or reason, thousands of wildly cheering spectators watched the sentence carried
out.

Juanita's crime was not simply that she had
killed a man. Her crime was that she had killed a
man, and she had dark skin. Juanita also danced at
the local fandango house, which to some made her
a prostitute. She was "Mexican"—which meant she
could also have been Chilean, Spanish, or Peruvian,
and she lived with a "Mexican" man. With the
growing Anglo animosity toward the people they
called "greasers," it was not hard for some hotheads
to fire up the mob.

Had Juanita been like Luzena Wilson—a white
woman doing "respectable" work, protected by a
white husband, and dressing in the long skirts of a
lady—there is no doubt Juanita would not have
become the only woman to be hung in the country
of the Mother Lode. Juanita went to her death saying she would have done the same thing again. She
was only twenty-three.

Nearly three decades later, a writer pondered the
meaning of Juanita's fate. "The right to make laws

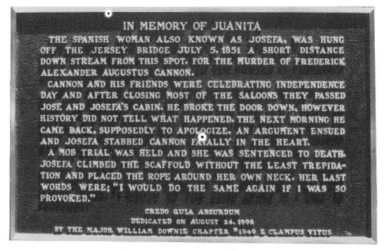

IN MEMORY OF JUANITA
THE SPANISH WOMAN ALSO KNOWN AS JOSEFA, WAS HUNG
OFF THE JERSEY BRIDGE JULY 5, 1851 A SHORT DISTANCE
DOWN STREAM FROM THIS SPOT. FOR THE MURDER OF FREDERICK
ALEXANDER AUGUSTUS CANNON.
    CANNON AND HIS FRIENDS WERE CELEBRATING INDEPENDENCE
DAY AND AFTER CLOSING MOST OF THE SALOONS THEY PASSED
JOSE AND JOSEFA'S CABIN. HE BROKE THE DOOR DOWN, HOWEVER
HISTORY DID NOT TELL WHAT HAPPENED. THE NEXT MORNING HE
CAME BACK, SUPPOSEDLY TO APOLOGIZE. AN ARGUMENT ENSUED
AND JOSEFA STABBED CANNON FATALLY IN THE HEART.
    A MOB TRIAL WAS HELD AND SHE WAS SENTENCED TO DEATH.
JOSEFA CLIMBED THE SCAFFOLD WITHOUT THE LEAST TREPIDA-
TION AND PLACED THE ROPE AROUND HER OWN NECK. HER LAST
WORDS WERE; "I WOULD DO THE SAME AGAIN IF I WAS SO
PROVOKED."

CREDO QUIA ABSURDUM
DEDICATED ON AUGUST 24, 1996
BY THE MAJOR WILLIAM DOWNIE CHAPTER #1849 E CLAMPUS VITUS

Plaque in Downieville, CA

necessarily entails the liability to suffer the penalties of their violation," he observed ever so sagely,
"and if women will have the former, she must
accept the latter."[10]

Juanita "suffered the penalties" of her "violation" sixty years before (non-Indian) women of
California could even vote, let alone make the laws!

Juanita was one of the many casualties of the
racism manifested in the Manifest Destiny that traveled with the American carnival parade. The gold of
the Mother Lode belonged to Americans, said
Governor Smith in 1849, contradicting the previous
governor's belief that it was "Anybody's Gold." In a
virtual legal vacuum, the doctrine of Might Makes
Right prevailed.

> **We were instruments known and
> recognized as Pioneers, and
> predestined to civilize the Pacific
> Coast. . . . Every member of a
> Christian nation should believe in an**

> **intelligent Creator and Ruler of the
> Universe. No people that has not this
> belief should be allowed admittance
> or a right of way over our boundary
> line. . . . Keep them out . . . I believe
> it is good policy to keep our country
> free from all entangling treaties with
> foreign nations.**
>
> —Mrs. Lee Whipple-Haslam

The legend of the Robin Hood-like bandit
Joaquin Murieta grew out of the anguish of Spanish-
speaking people in the Mother Lode. Joaquin may
have been a composite of angry young men; there
were plenty of them. According to one version of
his story, he was run off some claims, and whipped
by some Americans who also hanged his brother
and raped his wife (some say his mistress). He retal-
iated by robbing and murdering Anglos.

He—or they—based operations around Sonora
and Hornitos, in the southern mines, from 1850 to
1853. Some say women disguised as men rode with
him. The tale ended with the capture and decapita-
tion of a "Mexican" said to be Joaquin, but no one
knew for sure.

Mrs. Lee Whipple-Haslam, with all her biases,
defended Joaquin.

> **He was a peaceful, quiet miner I
> have seen him and talked with him.
> He never was known to molest
> women and children. I had a
> souvenir that once belonged to
> Joaquin—a silver saddle horn.**

For a while, various races and ethnic groups had
worked side by side. J.D. Borthwick, a Scotsman,

wrote about his travels through the Mother Lode. Before the Juanita incident, he had observed Italians, Frenchmen, Mexicans, and Americans working together peaceably near Downieville. And for a brief moment he saw a vision of what it could have been.

> **[T]his was the image that stuck in his mind, the multinational crew struggling to work in harmony and, in rare moments, succeeding. It was the acting out of a vague ideal J.S. had heard about as a child, the possibility of a world community.[11]**

But as more people went after less gold, the language began to set "foreigners" apart. Italians became "dagos," Frenchmen became "ingots" or "keskydees," Mexicans became "greasers." American committees of vigilantes began to organize riots, rumors, fights, claim jumping, "legal" appropriation of property, and roundups of "foreign troublemakers."

Taxation was one of the most effective tools of racism. When California became a state in April 1850, the new government imposed a tax of twenty dollars a month (later reduced) on every "foreign" miner. The tax targeted Mexicans, French, Chinese, and other non-English speakers, and fanned the flames of violence among the peoples who met on the carnival frontier.

Dame Shirley heaped contempt on Americans' attitudes, and quoted a Spanish expression:

> **Children speak in Italian, ladies speak in French, God speaks in Spanish, and the Devil speaks in English.**

It wasn't just ethnic violence. Back in Nevada City, a crazed mob nearly broke into Luzena Wilson's boarding house because they were after one of her boarders who had shot and killed a man in a card game. Turns out the gunman had disguised himself and was actually in the mob. He later sneaked out of town.

As Nevada City danced the quick two-step from the hopeful mind-your-own-business state to high carnival, many were led where they hadn't intended to go. Preachers hadn't ventured there yet to remind them of sinful ways, because, as Luzena observed, "[e]very man was too busy thinking of the preservation of his body to think of saving his soul . . .."

Men plunged wildly into every mode of dissipation to drown the homesickness so often gnawing at their hearts. They sang, danced, drank and caroused all night, and worked all day. They were possessed of the demon of recklessness, which always haunted the early mining camps. Blood was often shed, for a continual war raged between the miners and the gamblers. Nearly every man carried in his belt either knife or pistol, and one or the other flashed out on small provocation to do its deadly work.

—Luzena Wilson

Man breathed quicker and moved faster [in this environment]; the very windmills whirled here with a velocity that would make a

Hollander's head swim. And so like boys escaped from school, from supervision, the adventurer yielded to the impulse, and allowed the spirit within him to run riot.

—Hubert H. Bancroft

Part of the mad dance was the fickleness of fortune, wrote Luzena. Desperate poverty one day, riches beyond imagination the next. Speculation ran wild.

The fever and uncertainty of mining made the people grow old and haggard. They might dig, dig, dig, fruitlessly for days, making scarcely enough to keep body and soul together, and then disheartened, sell the worthless claim for enough provisions to last till they struck another camp.

A young man who decided to move on gave Luzena his claim he thought was exhausted. She sold it for one hundred dollars to a man who made ten thousand dollars from it before he left town.

It could make a person desperate. It could make a person crazy. And it kept happening. Dorinda Brennan came from New York to Grass Valley, near Nevada City, in 1856 with her husband, Michael. Sponsored by New York investors, Michael supervised operations of a company called Mount Hope while Dorinda took care of their three young children.

Mount Hope produced well until the vein ran out. More machinery and more shafts failed to produce the next vein Michael knew had to be there. Then water flooded the mine, ending Mount Hope,

Michael's dreams, Dorinda's hopes, and the stockholders' investments.

On a cold February day, neighbors discovered the bodies of the whole family—Michael, Dorinda, and their three children. Michael, desperate and humiliated, had poisoned his family and then himself. Their bodies now lie together in a Grass Valley cemetery.

Later, when the mine was reopened, men working at the bottom of the shaft found the vein—a few feet away from where Michael Brennan had given up his desperate search.

It was that kind of desperation that made the gamblers kings of high carnival. If a man couldn't pick up the gold of his dreams, maybe he could scrape together what he had and win big in a game. The "knights of the green table" were happy to give them the opportunity, and the gamblers became rich mining the miners. You could spot the gamblers because they were the best dressed men, the ones with the "biled" shirts.

The Brennan family gravesite (foreground), Grass Valley, CA

Luzena called the gamblers "generous, respect-
ful, and kindhearted." But that's not what Mrs. Lee
Whipple-Haslam called them. To her, they were part
of

> **an ever moving stream of human
> microbes from the cities—gun men,
> gamblers, blacklegs, and all the low
> class of the sporting element (men
> and women) . . .. They considered our
> hard-working miners lawful prey;
> and immediately introduced methods
> to reap the harvest.**

This "stream of microbes" gathered in the
saloons that sprang up as community centers everywhere in the Mother Lode. The saloons began as
tents, then shacks with "false fronts"—ornamental
facades pasted across the front to make them look
like two-story buildings. It's where the expression
"putting up a front" comes from, and Americans
were notorious for putting up a front on their
houses too.

Behind the false fronts were all kinds of "methods to reap the harvest" of miners' gold, and they all
involved the sale of liquor. Many offered free lunch-
es with purchase of booze. There was music and
dancing and camaraderie. The best lures were, of
course, women. It was the primary job of "pretty
waiter girls," hurdy-gurdy girls, and even prostitutes, to sell liquor.

Liquor loosened up many a miner's pocket and
purse, especially if he was down on his luck. And
what miner could resist a chance to sit down with
the beautiful dealer and play a friendly game of
cards?

French women arrived *en masse* in San

Francisco in 1850, and soon decorated the game
rooms as dealers. Dame Shirley wrote of a fabulous
San Francisco saloon where masked women
"graced, or disgraced" the tables.

Eliza Farnham wrote of her visit to a San
Francisco gaming room.

> **In one corner, a coarse-looking
> female might preside over a roulette-
> table, and . . . a Spanish or Mexican
> woman would be sitting at monte,
> with a cigarita in her lips. . . . In a
> very few fortunate houses, neat,
> delicate, and sometimes beautiful
> French women were every evening to
> be seen in the orchestra.**

The trend of women dealers traveled to the mining towns. In 1854, a young French "widow" grandly stepped from a stage coach in Nevada City and
soon was passing out handbills that advertised:

Madame Eleanore rented a vacant store and
announced that in her gaming parlor, "Only gentle-
men will be admitted. And only *vingt-et-un* [twen-
ty-one] will be played. Furthermore, I shall be the
dealer."

Madame Eleanore called her operation the "fanciest bar in California." It was fancy, all right, with its fifty-foot-long walls covered in scarlet cloth and imported French "art." Her operation soon expanded to a dozen tables for poker, monte, and faro, and space for dancing to the music of a fifteen-piece orchestra.

Within two years, the supply of miners and their gold slowed, and Madame Dumont closed up shop and took off for Some Place Else. Someone gave her the unfortunate nickname of "Madame Mustache," and it followed her from camp to camp throughout the West. Eleanore Dumont's story ended in her suicide in Sacramento, twenty-five years after she made her grand entrance in Nevada City.

Eleanore's Gaming Parlor must have hosted some fancy balls, where no doubt both dignified waltzes and wild fandangos were done.

Dame Shirley gave her account of a ball in Rich Bar's local bar room, which we may be sure was not as elegant as Madame Dumont's Parlor.

On ball nights the bar was closed, and everything was very quiet and respectable. To be sure, there was some danger of being swept away in a flood of tobacco juice; but luckily the floor was uneven, and it lay around in puddles, which with care one could avoid, merely running the minor risk of falling prostrate upon the wet boards, in the midst of a galopade.

Always, there was a shortage of women.
Europeans were the first to think of bringing women
to the Mother Lode as a business venture.

> The system of importing females from
> Germany, by contract, has been
> carried on with great profit . . ..
> Young girls are bought up, sent out
> here in ships, and have to serve a
> term of years to their master—no
> matter what labor may be required.[12]

Not all of the "imported" females were prostitutes. Mrs. Lee Whipple-Haslam remembered the
"hurdy-gurdy girls" from her childhood in a mining
camp.

> A hurdy-gurdy consisted of four girls
> with a man to play the violin. The
> girls were mostly German and more
> decent than the dance-house girls.
> Instead of drinking strong liquor,
> they drank something light. . . . Each
> and every dance cost the miner one
> dollar. . . . [The girls] would remain
> only a few days in a camp, then move
> to another.

> Bonnie are the hurdies O!
> The German hurdy-gurdies O!
> The daftest hour that e'er I spent
> Was dancing with the hurdies O!
> —popular miners' ditty

Once the Americans caught on to the profits of
importing women, professional procurers roamed
the East Coast and overseas, luring vulnerable tar-

gets with promises of respectable jobs with high pay and travel expenses. Eager young girls would find themselves trapped with no way to work off their debts but prostitution. Others came knowing they would be displaying or offering their bodies to get their gold.

The French prostitutes who flooded into California reigned at the top of the hierarchy of the *Demimonde*. In multilevel brothels, clients paid more the higher the floor, and those on the top level would be the French.

But even French chippies couldn't always stay on top, so to speak. A courtesan may quickly work her way to a top job, in a fancy parlor house, top floor. A fast life of liquor, drugs, and disease could just as quickly take her to the bottom floor and out the door to the sleazy cribs or the streets. Or she might become one of the "summer women" who migrated to the camps with the mining seasons.

The most common way out of prostitution was suicide. It still is, I am told.

The most exploited were the Chinese women and girls. This was a time when upper class Chinese women were hobbled by foot binding—a process that reduced their feet to curled stubs that measured perhaps three inches. Girls who escaped foot binding—called "Big Feet," were relegated to field work—if they were lucky. Unlucky ones were sold by desperate parents or stolen by Chinese agents, and shipped off to California—*Gum San* (Gold Mountain). Here, they were sold at auction for perhaps three hundred dollars in a land that was supposed to be free of slavery.

Highly-organized associations made obscene profits from the Chinese women. They would keep the younger ones in San Francisco, and send the older ones out to the mining camps, often moving them from town to town.[13]

In the Mother Lode masquerade, a lot was for show—the false fronts, the masks, the swagger of the newly-rich, the show of ankle and thigh and a lot more of the dance hall girls. And there was the show of circus and opera and theater as troupes of performers followed the miners around the Mother Lode.

[T]here was a traveling theatre to open for the first time in Marysville; and a mounted horseman was galloping through the streets, announcing, at the top of his voice, the programme of the evening's performance.

—Mrs. D.B. Bates

Lola Montez won fame as a dancer, actress, and countess. Though she adopted a flashy Spanish name, Maria Dolores Eliza Rosanna Gilbert, Countess of Landsfeld, was Irish. By the time she landed in Grass Valley, Lola had danced her way through much of the world, leaving a string of scandals and broken hearts behind. Her long list of lovers included Franz Liszt and Alexander Dumas. When she sashayed out of Bavaria, she left behind a bereft King Ludwig and his toppled kingdom.

Lola wowed audiences far and wide, more for her notoriety and flashing beauty than for her talent. Lola's most famous dance was the gyrating "spider dance," which she performed in all seriousness. In the Mother Lode, the miners laughed. Lola did not.

Lola had seen her better days when she decided to stay a while in Grass Valley. The town ladies were scandalized to have Lola Montez in their midst, and yet most anxious to receive an invitation to one of Madame Lola's salons. In her stately home, still standing on Mill Street, the hostess elegantly served her own receipt for German honey cakes, sandwiches, and tea laced with Jamaica rum.[14]

And she graciously gave her receipt for

LOLA'S FAVORITE SKIN LOTION

1/3 glycerin
1/3 rose water
1/3 strawberry juice

The woman with the wild, exotic past, though subject to occasional tantrums and other odd behavior, was tolerated—even respected—in Grass Valley. One newspaper editor recalled her good deeds.

> **Madam Lola (as she chose to be called while a resident of this town), although eccentric in some respects, did many acts indicative of a kind and benevolent disposition. We recall her riding many miles over the hills to carry food and medicine to a poor miner. More than once she watched all night at the bedside of a child whose mother could not afford to hire a nurse.[15]**

With her career on the wane, Lola tried a comeback in Australia, but the Aussies didn't appreciate her spider dance, singing, or acting. She returned to Grass Valley, retired from the theater, and went on the lecture circuit. She was forty years old when died in poverty in New York City.

In one of her lectures, Lola Montez described the classic dilemma of a nineteenth-century woman who longed to be free:

> **The great misfortune was that there was too much of me to be held within the prescribed and safe limits allotted**

Lola Montez
*Courtesy Searls
Historical Library,
Nevada City, CA*

**Lola's house, Grass
Valley, CA. A sign
on her house calls
Lola "a founder of
today's cosmetic
industry," and says
she brought together
many of the men
who founded the
area's quartz mining
industry.**

**to woman; but there was not enough
to enable me to stand securely beyond
the shelter of conventional rules.**[16]

Though Lola lived in Grass Valley for just two years, she left behind tantalizing stories that have become part of Mother Lode lore. She also gave Lotta Crabtree her start toward stardom, teaching her some dance steps and basics of show biz.

The little girl who laughed when she danced delighted the miners, who showered her with gold.

**She seemed tireless, a tiny bubbling
fountain of fun and quick life. . . .
Money rained upon the stage;
quarters, half-dollars, huge Mexican
dollars, a fifty-dollar gold slug, and a
scattering of nuggets.**[17]

Lotta Crabtree
*Courtesy Searls
Historical Library,
Nevada City, CA*

**Holbrooke Hotel, Grass Valley, CA,
frequented by both Lola Montez and Lotta Crabtree**

Lotta went on to delight audiences on stages around the world. She died at the age of eighty with a fortune of four million dollars.

Today as you stroll the streets of a Mother Lode town, the evening air gently blows sounds of past and present. A child's giggle at a street clown could be the laughter of little Lotta Crabtree dancing for gold. There's the sound of a fiddle, and some voices singing a rollicking miner's song.

There are tears, too—for a home far away, or a lost dream. But the tears aren't loud like the laughter.

That's the way most of the ones who were there remembered it.

CHAPTER SIX

Marie Pantalon:
The Lady Wore Pants!

We see by a San Francisco notice . . . that Marie Suize, better known in this vicinity as 'Madame Pantaloons' has been arrested in that city for wearing male apparel. She was left with a fine of five dollars by pledging herself to wear female toggery hereafter. This will afford the 'Women Suffrage Association' a splendid opportunity to hold a grand indignation meeting.
—Amador *Dispatch*, April 22, 1871

"Larry knows where all the bodies are buried," someone remarked when she recommended that I talk with Larry Cenotto, Amador County Archivist, about famous characters in his county.

Turns out he *doesn't* know where all the bodies are buried. He can't find the body he'd most like to find—that of Marie Suize, known in California as Marie Pantalon, or Madame Pantalon (Madame Pants).

According to her obituary, Marie Suize lies somewhere in the Catholic Cemetery of Jackson, in the central mining districts between Placerville and Sonora, but there's no grave marker. "Why should this celebrated, extraordinary, notorious woman be buried anonymously?" Larry wonders.

"Maybe St. Patrick's Parish agreed to bury her only if the grave was unmarked. After all, the church may have deemed her unworthy—sinful, an unmarried woman whose daily companions were men. Maybe a lesbian, certainly a cross-dresser. We know only the last is true."

What is known is that the lady was a miner and a mine owner, and she wore pants. As a miner and entrepreneur, she made a pile of money. As a gambler in stock speculations, she lost it. As a wearer of pants, she broke the rules and the law, and became famous.

What is known is that Marie Suize was among the thousands of French-speaking people lured to California by tales of gold. Marie was one of ten children of working-class parents who lived in the Thônes Valley in the duchy of Savoie, which later became part of France.

In 1850, at age twenty-six, Marie left home with her brother, nineteen-year-old Albert, and sailed to San Francisco. From there the pair made their way to the placer claims around Jackson, where some miners from their home valley were working claims.

Soon Marie was mucking around in the gravel with pick and shovel along with the men, dressed in the miner's uniform of canvas pants, muslin shirt, boots, and a hat. As this woman dressed as a man became known throughout the mining district, few people knew her real name. She was Marie, or Madame, Pantalon.

At a time when placer mining was giving way to more aggressive methods of coaxing out the gold, Marie and her compatriots made thousands of dollars placer mining in tunnel and gravel claims.

Working alongside fellow Savoyards, and sometimes supervising other miners, Marie became wealthy investing in mining claims and other properties. As a miner and mine owner, she defied tax collectors and ran off claim jumpers. In a decades-long partnership with Frenchman André Douet, she established an extensive vineyard and winery.

Among her later enterprises were a San Francisco wine shop and a store in Virginia City, Nevada. In both those cities, she was arrested for violating the prevailing laws against cross-dressing. And, California Gold Rush-style, she lost her money gambling on investments in Nevada's Comstock Lode.

Marie Suize died in 1892 after returning to the ranch she had owned with André Douet in Amador County. No one knows exactly where her body is buried.

This is what is known of Madame Pantalon. She left no known photograph or journal or other writings.

I think of Marie Suize as Everywoman who ever longed for adventure, ever dared to do something outrageous. Following, then, is the rest of Marie Pantalon's story as I imagine it to have been, in what I imagine to have been her own words.

Bonjour! Je m'appelle Marie. Marie Suize. That is my French name. In California, I am known as Marie Pantalon, or Madame Pantalon—Mrs. Pants! Don't laugh—I wear that name with much pride, because it is the name *mes amis* the miners gave to me when I started wearing pants so that I could work in the diggings for gold.

But, you may ask, why would a twenty-six-year-old woman with no husband take a dangerous trip across the sea to an unknown land? And how would she get to be known as Marie Pantalon?

One question at a time, please.

Well, I came from the duchy of Savoie, in what is now France. At the time Savoie was not a part of France, but it's OK to call me French. Everyone else does.

One thing you may *not* call me is a miner*ess*. I was a miner, a mine owner, and an entrepreneur. I was never a miner*ess*!

So, now that we have that straightened out, we may continue.

I lived in one of the most beautiful places in the world—in the Thônes Valley at the foot of the French Alps, with my family and friends. *C'est magnifique, non?*

Mais non. Times were very hard all around us. Sickness was everywhere and crops were failing and people were hungry. But at least we had enough to eat. And that was because the women worked so hard!

My own mother was one of those women. She had ten children and all I ever saw her do was work. Wash, cook, milk the cows, churn the butter, sew, clean, work in the fields. She took care of everyone but herself. I did not want that life for myself! But in my village, it seemed to be the only—how do you say it?—respectable thing for a woman to do.

Pour moi, I wanted something different. I wanted

to make a good life for myself. And the only way I could do that was to make good money—like I could perhaps if I were a man. I dreamed of a new life in Paris. Ah, Paris! But I was a mountain woman, used to outdoor work. The only work for a single woman in Paris was to be a maid or a sewing lady or a factory girl. Or, of course, a prostitute. Ooh la, la, you say. *Mais non*—not for me.

And—not to forget—in Paris, I might land in the middle of a revolution! In Paris and in cities all over Europe, poor people were revolting against the rich people. The poor people worked long hours in filthy conditions for scraps of food and miserable places to live so that the rich could live like kings. It was not fair, *non?*

Liberté! Egalité! Fraternité! That's what the poor people fought for, and many of them were women. *Mais oui*, in the Revolution of 1789, it was mainly women who marched to Versailles Palace waving brooms and pitchforks, swords and pistols. They demanded bread and soap for their children, and fair wages. Well, wouldn't you?

Women were fighting again in the revolution of 1848, and they demanded the right to vote—just like the women of Seneca Falls, New York, in the same year.

And what did the women get? They did not get *liberté* or *egalité*. With each revolution, ruling men took away the rights of women so that we could not even form clubs or take part in politics! In fact, women were grouped with children, criminals, and the insane, and had no rights.

What would you do? Wouldn't you want to be free?

Well, about this time we began to hear the news from California. *De L'or! De L'or!* Gold! Gold in California!

Look at this poster that came out in France in 1849. *"DES MILLIONS POUR UN SOU! MINES D'OR DE LA CALIFORNIE,"* it says. "Millions for a Penny, Gold Mines of California."

I will translate a bit for you.

> **Oh you, who go through the large city with boots eternally worn down, who search for the most obscure coins, the most ignored in your innumerable houses, who find strength to earn the black bread and meager soup which allows you to see tomorrow! On to the gold mines of California!**

Très poètique, non? It goes on . . .

> **Oh you, young women, who, without dowries, would be eternally without a husband! . . . Oh you, singers, vagabonds, escape artists, entertainers . . . Jews, usurers, stockbrokers, solicitors, bailiffs, business men, lawyers, lepers of humanity . . . you who spend your life paddling in dirty water like ducks . . . On to the gold mines of California! Go!**

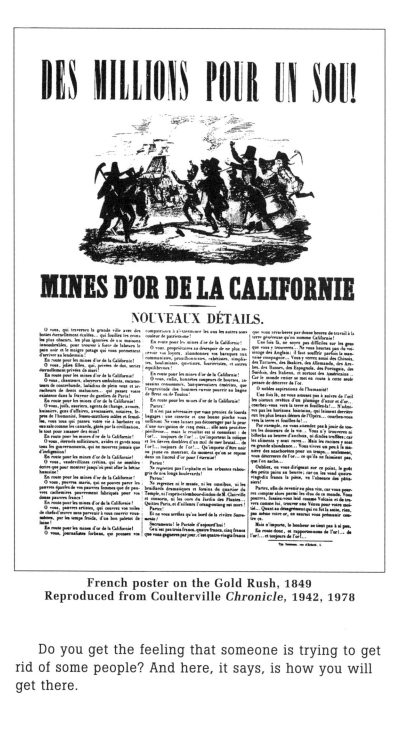

French poster on the Gold Rush, 1849
Reproduced from Coulterville *Chronicle*, 1942, 1978

Do you get the feeling that someone is trying to get rid of some people? And here, it says, is how you will get there.

It is not necessary to take heavy bags.
A money box and a good pickax will be
sufficient for you. Don't be discouraged
by the fear of a five-month journey. It
may be perilous but the result is very
consoling: gold! Always gold! Never
mind colic and fevers doubled with
sickness from the brutal sea. *De l'or!*
Toujours de l'or! **Gold! Always gold!**
Never mind being black or yellow in
death; the moment you die you will be
in a shroud of gold for eternity!
Partez! **Go!**

It says not to expect to find niceties and enjoy an
easy time, and no daydreaming, bird watching, or fine
cuisine française—just keep digging.

Curious as this poster may seem, it does describe
the strangeness of *les mines d'or de la Californie!*

De l'or! Toujours de l'or! It was all I could think of.
I dreamed golden dreams. If I could get there, I would
be rich! I would be free!

The French caught the gold fever even before
the Yankees did. All over my country, men organized
companies to sail to California. By 1852, as many as
thirty thousand *Français* had gone to the gold
fields.

People were leaving our Thônes Valley for many
different places because times were so hard. Even
children had to go to the cities to work as chimney
sweeps!

I watched men from our valley leaving for
California. And I wanted to go too!

Women were among those who left for California,
even in 1849 and 1850. Many of them were prostitutes
from Paris. One California newspaper reported that the

Chimney-sweep children leaving the Thônes Valley and their family. A man who became rich in America returns with a suitcase full of gold.
Drawing by André Burnier,
Courtesy Collection of Les Amis du Val de Thônes, France

hookers were "a host of fallen angels who go to purify themselves in a bath of gold."

Actually, Louis Napoléon Bonaparte, alias Napoléon III, wanted to get rid of prostitutes and revolutionaries he did not want around—just as the poster said.

You see, he did a very clever thing. After the people lost their bloody revolution of 1848, he declared that *he* was President of France. And then he used the people's dreams of California gold to get their attention on something besides their quarrels with the government.

When the President heard of *l'or*, he and his police cooked up a lottery scheme called *"L'Ingot d'Or,"* and grandly promised bars of solid gold to the winners. And he said the profits would go to help thousands of "deserving poor" to reach California and start a new life.

Well, he pocketed most of the lottery money. And in 1851, he started shipping out *les misérables*— revolutionaries, criminals, prostitutes, and pimps, and— you may be sure—strong-minded women. And then, not satisfied with being President, Louis Napoleon announced that he was now Emperor!

Very smart cookie, as we say here in America, *non?*

And so, many of the French people leaving for California in 1851 and 1852 were the very people Napoléon III—excuse me—the Emperor—wanted to get rid of. That's why no *Français* ever said he came to California during those years. They were called ingots, and it was not a compliment.

In the mine fields the Americans often called us "keskydees" and "parleyvoos."[1] They would hear us say *"Qu'est-ce qu'il dit?"* for "What are you saying?" And of course they all asked us, *"Parlez vous Français?"*

As for me, my dream came true. In 1850, I was on a ship with my brother Albert, bound for California! Now please remember. That was before *L'Ingot!*

Of course, most people who came from France were ordinary people, like my brother Albert and me. Frenchmen organized more than eighty societies and companies to come to California.[2]

My brother Albert was only nineteen when we left. In our family, Albert was a younger brother, you see, and so he could not inherit any of the family's meager money. As a woman, I could not inherit either, of course. And so together Albert and I set forth to face the sea and find our own fortune.

Our ship was crowded with people, many of them sick. We were only seasick, but some took fever and died. I will never forget the sight and sound as a dead child, wrapped in a quilt, was thrown into the sea, its tomb.

After five months, *mon Dieu*, how can I tell you what greeted us when we stepped off the ship in San Francisco Bay? The harbor was crowded with ships, with many people living on them, especially what we politely called *filles de joie* [girls of joy].

The sounds of San Francisco rang in my ears. Miners in their dirty clothes and ragged beards crowded around the ships, yelling for relatives or friends or wives or sweethearts or harlots. Men were waving things to sell—gold pans, gold machines, and passage to the gold fields. Mexican men yelled invitations to the next bull fight. Brass bands blasted the air.

San Francisco then was becoming a city. What a potpourri of shacks and tents and brick buildings! And the streets! You could not really call them streets. They were long mud holes, full of things you can't imagine, and *grand* piles of bottles and cans and miners' worn-out clothes, and swarms of rats feasting on it all![3]

I was glad Albert was with me as we made our way through a sea of men. Albert was not only my brother. He was my friend and my protector. More than once he saved me from men who would have done me harm. People often mistook him for my husband, and that was OK with me.

I saw a few women, but not many who looked like ladies. Imagine my amazement to see a prostitute in men's clothes racing by on her horse, splashing mud all over. Other fancy women plodded through the mud wearing the latest Paris fashions.

Oh, the jangle of languages! There was Spanish, Dutch, German, Italian, Norwegian, Turkish, Swedish, Danish, English, and French, of course, and many I did not know what they were.

But even with all those languages, it seemed to me that San Francisco was trying to be like Paris. *C'etait drôle!* A merchant would set up a tent with a fancy sign and that would be a French café! Already they were importing items from France—wines, champagnes, brandies, sardines, and olives. And there were French gambling houses and theaters, and even French circuses!

I soon discovered that the men chased after anything that was French, especially women. Mind you, I was wearing the dress I had saved for my arrival in California. It had long sleeves, a high neck, and full skirts with petticoats that were respectably below the ankles. And I wore my hair pulled back and pinned down, neat and ladylike. But it made no difference.

About the only place one could walk was on the plank streets in front of the saloons and hotels. When word got around that I was coming, the men poured out of the saloons onto the plank streets and crowded around me, calling and whistling and stomping. And when they learned that I was French, they went wild. They followed me around, calling "Ooh, la la!" And

"Voulez-vous coucher avec moi?" Those were the only French words some of them knew—"will you sleep with me?"

Excusez-moi? Because I was French, they assumed I was a harlot!

I learned that French women were working in the gambling houses. They were dealers and dancers and "pretty waiter girls," and, of course, *les grandes horizontales.* The French hookers usually got the highest prices. I heard that many women who just a month before were streetwalkers in Paris, now were making several hundred dollars a night in gold!

We were not in San Francisco for long. I tried to find work that I wanted to do, but it was no use. The only jobs for women were to serve men—doing their washing or cooking, dancing for them, selling them liquor or luck, or their bodies.

Non. I wanted to get close to the gold. So Albert and I bought supplies and set out for Jackson's Creek, where we hoped to find some of our countrymen.

We took a steamboat to Sacramento, and then made our way on mules through mud and dirt until finally we reached the camp. I was so filthy I just wanted to hide. But I didn't see any place that looked clean. All I could see were ragged tents, shacks, and mud.

We found our fellow Savoyards, and many Frenchmen. They wore filthy clothes, scruffy beards, and muddy faces. I could not keep from laughing. Under their ragged hats I recognized the hairy faces of men we knew, André Douet and Jean Allard.

The men were so glad to see us they crowded around us and welcomed us with shouts and handshakes. They even took off their hats to me and bowed!

After they quieted down, the men told Albert how glad they were to have another man to help them dig for the gold. And they needed him to help defend it too. The Americans were saying that the French were clannish, and they didn't like it that the French seemed to have struck some of the richest claims. Mind you, the Americans did not like the French miners, but they loved French prostitutes and French things! How do you explain that?

The miners stared at me. One of them reached out and put in my hand a piece of gold the size of an acorn. I stared at it, turning it over and over. At last! *L'or!* I could almost feel the warmth of its glow. The miner told me I could have it. And he said there was plenty of gold for me in exchange for washing and cooking.

The men started cheering! At last a woman! At last there was someone to make bread and pies, wash their grubby shirts and filthy pants, fix their meals, darn their socks! Someone to wash their pots and pans, and haul their bath water! They started dancing around and yelling, and singing a song they learned from the Americans:

> **We miss thee at the washing-tub,**
> **When our sore and blistered digits**
> **Have been compelled to weekly rub—**
> **Bringing blues, hysterics, fidgets.**
> **'Tis then we miss thy timely aid—**
> **Oh, do have pity gentle maid!**[4]

I looked around. I did not see another woman. *Tragique.* In my mind I could see nothing but hungry miners demanding their pies and bread and bath water. Suddenly I was imagining that I was buried under waves of their filthy clothes.

So I did something very crazy. I turned to the miners, and very clearly and very loudly, I said *"NON! You have been taking care of yourselves up to now. You can keep on doing it!"*

Mon Dieu! I think if my brother had not been there, the men would have kicked me out of the camp.

"My dream, too, is in the diggings," I told them. "And that's where I will go."

The men were silent. They could not believe what they had heard. And they just walked away, grumbling about strong-minded women.

But I was determined. The next day, I went out to the diggings beside my brother. I wore a skirt, of course, knowing that I should at least try to look like a lady in a place where women were not welcome. Before I could start digging, the mud filled my shoes and soaked into my skirts. I could hardly even get to the gravel because my skirts kept getting in the way. The men just laughed.

By the end of the day, my skirt was torn, and my shoes ruined. Back at our shack, I was so frustrated and angry, I threw them all away. Out the window they went! I knew then that the only thing to wear in the diggings was what the men wore—pants!

The next morning I eagerly jumped into my brother's extra pants and shirt. I pinned up my long hair and tucked it under a dirty hat. Finally, I put on the tall boots I had bought in San Francisco. Alongside Albert, I strode right through the mud. I could move! I felt like dancing!

I caused quite a stir. The way the men looked at me you would think I was stark naked! It was a shocking thing to do, to wear pants. Not only that, it was illegal. *Oui!*

The gold fields may have been a place of freedom—
for the men. But just as in France, there were laws
here against what they called "cross-dressing." Mind
you, it was legal for a woman to bare her legs—and
more—in the dance halls. But it was *not* legal for a
woman to *cover* her legs with pants!

But I did not care what the law said, or what
anyone thought. Let the men stare! Let them arrest me!
I would wear what I needed to wear to do my work.

That night, when I returned to camp, I took the
final step. I cut off my long hair so it wouldn't get in
my way. Then I looked in my *petite*, scratched mirror.
The woman who looked back at me was, for the first
time in her life, free.

And so I entered the mining life. It was the hardest,
hottest, coldest work that you can imagine. Some days
I stood in icy water up to my knees all day as I washed
water through sand in my pan over and over to
separate out the gold. Day after day I shoveled out
gravel and carried it to long toms and sluice boxes to
wash out the gold.

The work was not only hard, but lonely. The men
did not know what to think of a woman working
beside them, wearing pants. The few women who
came to the camps also did not know what to think
about me. Most of the women who were ladies stayed

away from me, simply because I wore pants! A lady was not supposed to do that! But some of the prostitutes accepted me. Because we were all together, it seemed, in defying the rules.

It was hard living in the camps. In our little shacks we were cold much of the time. And we did not often have fruits and vegetables, or time to cook. There was garbage in the streets and dirt and mud everywhere. And so we had much sickness—scurvy and malaria, and even cholera.

Oh, I was grateful my mother did not know how Albert and I lived! How I longed for home, and clean sheets, and hot food. I tried to make things better for my countrymen in the camp. I tended many of them when they were sick, and at least once a month I was able to prepare a special dinner for them. We would eat good food, prepared as at home. Would you like one of my *recettes*—or receipts, as you call them—that I prepared for the men?

Here is a *recette* that pleased my countrymen.

Potted Cheese
Pound about a pound and a half of cheddar cheese in a mortar and add about a fourth of a coffee mug of sherry. Mix and flavor with nutmeg, salt and pepper. This makes a fine spread on bread or crackers.[5]

On those evenings we would sing songs from our country. Oh, those times made us long for our country, and our village, and the friends and family we left behind.

Au clair de la lune,
Mon ami, Pierrot,
Prête moi ta plume,

Pour écrire un mot.
Ma chandelle est morte,
     Je n'ai plus de feu,
  Ouvre moi ta porte,
     Pour l'amour de Dieu.

And so the miners became *mes amis* and
companions and protectors. And they began to call me
"Marie Pantalon." It was a title I earned, and I wore it
proudly. Wearing pants, I felt so free that I never
wanted to put on skirts again.

I was not the only woman who panned for gold. I
was told that before 1849, many families panned for
gold. There were Indian families, and families from
Sonora, Mexico. Some women from Sonora, brought
teams of men with them and worked in diggings not
far to the south of us. And another woman, who looked
much too old for such hard work, panned gold on her
own claim near Jackson Gate.

A few American ladies panned for gold beside
their husbands, but most of them did it for fun. Men
liked having ladies and children visit the diggings,
and let them keep whatever they happened to find.
But most ladies were not serious enough about it to
wear pants, not like "Marie Pantalon."

Even though mining was the hardest work I've ever
done, looking for l'or was like a hunt for treasure! I
never knew when I was going to find a fine lump of
gold glowing in the bottom of the sluice box. *Quel bel
or!* Often I would pick up a nugget and it seemed that
its warmth would just go right through me.

The work became harder and more dangerous for
us. As more seekers of *l'or* crowded into the mine
fields, trouble followed. Remember I told you that the
Americans were jealous of the French? Well, they were
jealous of everyone foreign, but especially the French.
But we defended our rights.

At French Hill, French and Americans nearly went to war before the French consul stepped in. The French kept most of their claim, and between 1851 and 1853, they took out more than ten million dollars! *C'est la guerre!*

In 1850, right after California became a state, the lawmakers started to tax all foreign miners. Twenty dollars a month! They charged the taxes mainly to try to force out the Mexicans, the Chinese, and us French. We French led the fight against it. The lawmakers backed down, but later brought back the taxes, though not as much.

How we hated those taxes! I remember the day the "Tax Collector" came to the diggings and demanded that I pay taxes! *Moi! Une femme!* As a woman, I refused to pay because the taxes were only supposed to be for the men.

Do you know what he did? He knocked me to the ground! *Vraiment!* I came up fighting, and the other miners came to help me, so I wasn't hurt much.

"Well, if you are a woman," the tax man yelled, "why in the hell not dress like one?"

It was obvious to everyone that if I dressed as a woman, I would not be able to get *l'or.* That was the whole point, of course. Later I paid their petty tax. But I had stood up to that pesky tax man.

In the Jackson Gate district, I hired men to help me tunnel into the gravel beds. And we found gold—a lot of gold. Always, I wore my miner's clothes, and I worked with my pick and shovel like the rest of them.

My most famous fight was on Humbug Hill. How well I remember! One night, some Canadians moved into one of my tunnels, so they could take it over. So I simply set up camp at the tunnel entrance, bed and all, with two pistols and a soup bowl full of red pepper.

We plugged up the ventilation hole so the trespassers would have to come out. "You'd better come

out peacefully and never come back," I yelled, "or
you'll get a faceful of pepper! And I have guns to back
me up!"

They came out. Then we unplugged the hole and
our men went into the tunnel and worked. For eight
days and nights I stayed at my post, armed with
pepper and guns. And the claim jumpers never came
back.

How I loved that gold! It made me rich! Soon I
owned shares in mines and diggings with names like
Gopher Flat, New York Gulch, and Wildcat Tunnel.

Albert returned to France, as he had planned, and
took with him much of the money we made. I traveled
back to France too, and I tried to convince my sisters
to come to California with me. But they did not share
my dreams. I was in love with *l'or* and my freedom,
and so I returned to California and never went back to
France.

By the mid-'fifties, mining was becoming harder,
and companies were coming in with equipment to dig
deeper into mountains and streambeds, and to free the
gold from the rocks. We built water channels and
flumes to divert the water, and bridges to connect
roads. In 1869, I was the only woman to sign my name
on a petition to fund some bridges. You see? There is
my miner name: Marie Suize Pantalon! And look—right
above mine is the signature of *mon ami* Jean—which
he spelled "John"—Allard.

In the 1860s, I bought some land with my *confrère* André Douet. We mined gold from that land, and then brought from the soil another kind of gold—grapes to make our beloved wines. We French and some Italians were pioneers in making the wine and brandy of Amador County. In the county census of 1870, I was one of six vintners listed. I had a bigger inventory than anyone else listed—five thousand gallons!

For Sale.

 THIRTY-FIVE SPIRIT PIPES, 20 of them new; 15 of them have been in use but are in complete order. Also, 9 Casks holding from 600 to 800 gallons each. The Casks are supplied with gates for the purpose of entering to clean them.

  For particulars, apply at Madame Pantaloon's ranch, near Slabtown!   jy15-2m

—Amador *Ledger,* 1872

I was always looking for opportunities to expand my wealth, and so I opened a wine shop in San Francisco, and a liquor store and wholesale house in Virginia City, Nevada.

Then I saw another opportunity to become even richer. I could double my money, perhaps buy more land, and send more money back to France! And so I bought into stocks in the Comstock Lode of silver and gold that was just opening up in Nevada. But the stocks didn't pan out, as we say. Hoping to get my money back, I kept investing. In the end, I lost one hundred and fifty thousand dollars gambling in mining stocks.

Well, I was rich several times, and I was poor—several times. But through it all, I still had the land and vineyards with André, and that is where I retired until the end of my life.

Looking back, I believe that what I left behind was my name, and my story—the story of "Madame Pantalon." I loved the freedom of wearing my pants and boots, but it got me in trouble a few times. California was an unruly place during the Gold Rush. But just as in France, women still were not free to dress and behave as they pleased.

Many cities and towns had laws against "cross-dressing." *Vive la différence*, I guess. Of course, some brilliant men noted that the laws did not discriminate against women, because men could not wear women's clothes either! Now tell me, how many men would want to wear those heavy, prison-like skirts and petticoats that women were expected to wear?

I never tried to hide the fact that I was a woman. I was proud to be a woman. But I often wondered how many other miners and wanderers who roamed the Mother Lode were really women in disguise.

I had to get special permission from Amador County to wear pants as a miner. So in my own area, I could move freely. But when I traveled to San Francisco and Virginia City, Nevada, I ran into trouble. I drove my own wagon to Virginia City, wearing pants, with a rifle over my knees because one never knew when trouble might arrive.

I had gone to Virginia City to check on my store. The male gossips—the ones who sat around and watched everything that went on—saw me drive into town and reported me to the city fathers.

They arrested me and accused me of wearing pants! They were about to pass some sort of sentence on me when I drove my wagon out of town.

Then, in 1871, I was arrested in San Francisco for the same terrible thing—wearing pants! You can read all about it in the Virginia City *Territorial Enterprise.*

You know how some men feel compelled to report on how a woman looks? Well, here is how the Virginia City writer judged me:

> **It is said that she looks much better in male than female habiliments; we should suppose so. She had not the face or figure to set off a Grecian bend. She was sailor built. She will be apt to get out of San Francisco and into Amador County and her breeches as speedily as possible.**

Sailor built! *Zut alors!*

Eh bien. I thought I could avoid trouble in San Francisco if I applied for a permit to wear pants. I told the judge that I had worn pants for eighteen years working in the mines, and had even traveled in Europe in pants.

The writer went on to say that other "Sole Traders" were "uneasy" about me. Let me explain. Sole Traders were married women who operated their own businesses. They could keep their own money under the Sole Traders Act. This law was inspired by old Spanish laws that—unlike traditional US law—allowed married women to keep their own property. It turned out that the other women wanted the choice to wear pants as I did!

Well, we can't have women with the freedom to dress as they like, now can we? So I was arrested and fined five dollars for wearing "male apparel." And worse, I was instructed to wear the "proper habiliments" of my sex.

"This will afford the 'Women Suffrage Association' a splendid opportunity to hold a grand indignation meeting," wrote the clever reporter.

My adventures stirred up quite a protest in the Woman Suffrage Association, which organized a special meeting to express their indignation at such a woman of iniquity—*moi!*

Yes, many of the ladies who campaigned in California for women to vote did not approve of my pants. Though some of the Sole Traders were on my side, they did not dare say so in public because they would lose business. And the suffrage ladies were afraid that they would lose their fight for the right to vote if it looked as though women wanted to be free instead of using their power to "civilize" the men. Many of the suffrage ladies thought of me as an embarrassment.

Well, by the time I returned to Amador County (in pants, by the way), news had traveled there of my arrests. And, unfortunately for me, there had been a fuss on the East Coast about the arrest of Dr. Mary Edwards Walker. This brave woman had served as a doctor during the Civil War and won a Congressional Medal of Honor! She had been caught strolling the streets of New York decked out in a top hat and a cutaway. *Très* shocking!

Some men in Amador County thought they had to keep up with the big boys in New York, and so they brought me to trial in my own home town! But others came to my defense. "If [some of the men] were to wear Mother Hubbards, I would object as they are very rotund," said one. "But if Madame Suize wants to wear pants, let her!"

Another man ended the discussion by pointing out, "We're wasting time, Judge. Let's adjourn and go hunting." And they did.

Mais oui, I had more support among the men of Amador County than among the women. I was often lonely for female company. I think the other women were jealous and considered me a threat since I dressed as a man and worked as a man.

La Liberté was a hard thing for a woman. Women were not supposed to desire freedom. If we did, and we pursued it, people laughed at us. And we were lonely. So I can't blame those women who condemned me. They were only protecting themselves.

Yes, I found freedom wearing pants. But you may be surprised to learn that I did own some rather elegant ladies' clothes. I especially prized a black velvet dress, buttoned with—what else?—five-dollar gold pieces! And my night clothes were of fine cloth, embroidered and beribboned.

And who would have known of my night clothes? My business partner, André Douet? My rumored lover, Jean Allard? Perhaps another woman? Or the mysterious Sebastien, my rumored husband?

Eh bien. That is one secret I have taken to my grave.

By the way, do you wonder? Wherever my grave is, do you think I was buried wearing a dress—or pantalon?

C'est le mystère.

CHAPTER SEVEN

'Leaving Nothing to Show That You Are a Woman'

> **When a woman unsexes her mind,**
> **and enters upon pursuits for which**
> **she was never intended, [she]**
> **outrages all those finer sentiments**
> **which go to make society endurable**
> **and the family circle desirable.**
> —The Sacramento *Bee,* 1864[1]

The Cult of True Womanhood dictated that a lady be by gosh *different* from a man. It wasn't just a social rule. In many parts of the world, it was the law. Then, as now, defying this law could bring much worse consequences than fines and ridicule.

Why, if a woman wears pants, it means she's thinking thoughts that are unladylike, unpatriotic, anti-family, and downright subversive!

Marie Pantalon may have been inspired by some uppity women of France. In the fifteenth century, none other than the young French heroine Joan of Arc got in trouble for questioning male authority— and for wearing pants. Marie Pantalon, by the way, was called "The Joan of Arc of Amador County" in a French newspaper in San Francisco.

After Jeanne d'Arc fought the English and paved the way for Charles, the Dauphin, to be King of

France, she was brought to trial. Church authorities found her guilty—not of fighting, nor of witchcraft, as many believe. She was pronounced guilty of heresy—acting as an independent woman by following what she believed to be "God's authority" rather than man's. Her final charge:

> **[Y]ou have continually used male
> dress . . . wearing your hair short . . .
> leaving nothing to show that you are
> a woman.**[2]

They burned Jeanne d'Arc at the stake in 1431. She was only nineteen.

Other French women "left nothing to show they were a woman." They weren't burned at the stake, but they, like Jeanne d'Arc, inspired other women by defying male authority and the law (pretty much the same thing).

French novelist George Sand (Aurore Dupin) was one. In the 1830s, she wore men's pants and a man's name. George Sand's mother inspired her daughter to wear pants when she told how she and her sister in earlier years had dressed like men in order to save money and "go everywhere."[3] And so, George Sand put on pants and boots and "went everywhere" disguised as a man. She especially loved her boots.

**I'd gladly have slept in them I
dashed back and forth across Paris
and felt I was going around the
world. . . . I was out and about in all
weather, came home at all hours, was
in the pit of all the theatres. Nobody
heeded me, or suspected my
disguise.[4]**

In 1857, French painter Rosa Bonheur petitioned
Paris police to wear pants in public. Pants were
much more practical in places where she studied
her subjects, like slaughter houses. And, dressed as
a man, she didn't have to worry about sexual
advances when she went out in public. She took to
wearing pants all the time, except for official
occasions.[5]

In California, Marie Pantalon wasn't the only
woman who wore pants. A brave few wore
bloomers, the baggy pants introduced at the Seneca
Falls Convention of 1848. Silly as they may have
looked, for some women, especially on the
California Trail, bloomers offered a way for a
woman to move more freely and still be a lady. But
women finally gave up on bloomers because wearing them wasn't worth the ridicule they inspired.

One of the most famous of California women
pants wearers was Charley Parkhurst. Disguised as a
man, she was a stagecoach driver—one of the best in
a dangerous business. For example, there was
always the danger of robbers on the road—like
Dutch Katy, who dressed as a man for her trade as a
road bandit.[6]

Charley learned to handle horses working at a
livery stable after she ran away from a
Massachusetts orphanage disguised as a boy. When
California Stage Lines began operating in the early

1850s, the owners sent for Charley. She wore home-made shirts, jeans, a double-breasted coat, a wide leather belt, leather boots, and a hat. And she always wore fancy leather gloves—perhaps to hide her small hands.

Charley drove a six-horse stage, and some said that to watch her drive was "poetry in motion." She was fearless on the road, they said. Known as "One-Eyed Charley," she wore a black eye patch over her injured eye after she was kicked in the face by a horse she was shoeing. One time she raced over a flooded bridge just before it collapsed.

Stagecoach from Ione to Jackson
Courtesy Calaveras County Historical Society, San Andreas, CA

Asked how she could see the road through all
the dust she encountered when it wasn't raining,
she replied, "I listen for the wheels to rattle, then I
know I'm on hard ground. If they don't rattle, I look
to see if the road's still there."[7]

Opinion is divided on whether Charley ever
drank or gambled, but some said she could outcuss
a lot of other drivers. She stayed away from women,
apparently because they kept falling in love with
her. Mothers waited for Charley's stage so their children would be safe, so the story goes. But still, the
ride was an adventure:

> **Spinsters fair and forty,**
> **maids of youthful charms,**
> **Suddenly are cast into their**
> **neighbors' arms;**
> **Children shoot like squirrels,**
> **darting through a cage—**
> **Isn't it delightful, riding in a stage?**[8]

Charley became known as the first woman to
vote, because she cast her vote regularly as Charley
Parkhurst, Stage Driver. No one knew that she was a
woman.

Elsa Jane Forest Guerin was another famous
woman pants wearer, and one of several women
known as "Mountain Charley." She disguised herself as a man to hunt down her husband's killer
(which she never succeeded in doing). Twice in her
adventures in disguise, she traveled the California
Trail to "the distant land of gold."

Elsa Jane wrote of a woman and two children her
party had taken into a wagon. She found them in a
tent, near death. The husband and father had gone
ahead to find feeding ground for their animals, but
never returned. They later found him dead on the

desert. Elsa Jane's heart went out to the woman—
alone with two children, everything gone. The
woman desperately needed a woman's care, and
Elsa Jane longed to fill that need.

> **I longed to disclose to her my sex,**
> **and minister to her in that manner in**
> **which only one woman can to**
> **another—yet I did not dare to, and I**
> **was forced to give her only that**
> **rough consolation which befitted my**
> **assumed character.**[9]

Mountain Charley apparently wasn't as strong as
Marie Pantalon, because she wrote in her autobiography that she "did not find my strength sufficient
for the [mining] business." So she went on to
Sacramento and started a mule packing business
and did very well.

"I could go where I chose," wrote Elsa Jane. "I
could do many things which while innocent in
themselves, were debarred by propriety from association with the female sex."

Some women periodically wore pants as a matter
of convenience. Rosa Bruschi, a Coulterville mother, storekeeper, and midwife, sometimes put on her
husband's clothes and packed a pistol to ride horseback on a mission to deliver a baby if the roads were
too muddy for horse and buggy.[10]

We'll never know how many women passed as
men in the California Gold Rush. It wasn't hard to
hide who you were; people didn't ask many
questions.

The "men" riding mules into town may well be
prostitutes plying their trade from mining camp to
mining camp. Some of the riders with the infamous
Mexican bandit Joaquin Murieta were women dis-

guised as men. And, in addition to Marie Pantalon, probably there were other miners who were women wearing men's clothes.

An Indian woman known as Toypurina led raids against invading Spaniards during the mission building days. You can bet she wasn't wearing skirts.[11]

At least one other woman besides Marie Pantalon was arrested for wearing pants. Eliza Ann Hurd Dewolf was part of the Spiritualist movement that was born in the eastern US and came west, especially to California. The idea was that women's rights were a divine right, superceding men's laws.

Eliza Dewolf had the nerve to ride a horse astride. And when she occasionally put on men's clothes, she inspired comments such as this newspaper item: "None but the old and ugly are jealous of the rights or the costume of men."

Eliza Dewolf was not very attractive, and she chose an unfortunate costume that led to her arrest in 1866, before Marie Pantalon was nabbed. Outfitted for a public lecture, Eliza Dewolf wore a bobtail coat over a short petticoat, which was worn over pants, topped with a hat with side veil and feather. The press had a fit.

"Any woman who appears on the street arrayed in a suit of men's clothes, insults the whole sex . . . ," huffed one writer.

None other than the famous writer Bret Harte expressed his alarm:

> **[Californians] cannot afford to accept any innovation which tends to lower the standard of female modesty, to make her more masculine and *confident* [emphasis added].[12]**

Eliza Dewolf and her husband tried and failed to get the city of San Francisco to strike down the ridiculous dress ordinance. In the process, Eliza was sentenced to jail. She was released, but the ordinance still stood, as Marie Pantalon would later find out.

After Eliza Dewolf's encounter with the law, at least one newspaper writer had it right. He wrote:

Any judge who would send a woman to jail for wearing short dresses must be a consummate leather-head.[13]

In California and elsewhere, there were plenty of leather-heads to go around.

CHAPTER EIGHT

What of the Children?

Thus it chanced that I, the youngest and weakest of those who had gone to California, alone returned to Missouri.

—Martha (Jennie) Ross Gentry

Most children bound for the Mother Lode traveled the overland trail—the path of families. Between 1841 and 1865, as many as forty thousand children traveled the trails westward with their families.[1]

For many children, the Mother Lode—and the getting there—was a grand adventure, and many came through the experience with remarkable resilience. But of all the people who met in the Mother Lode, the children were the most vulnerable. While many were treasured, some were horribly exploited, and others left alone. Parents or guardians could die, or split up, or leave a child with a stranger.

Here, in this land of carnival and whimsy where anything could happen, children often were like leaves floating in the wind. Whether or not they landed safely depended on luck, and on drifting into the hands of the right person.

In perpetual memory of a child who died on the emigrant
trail, visitors leave teddy bears and toys in a crib beside a
monument to Julian Albert Apperson, who was not yet three
when he died less than ten miles from Nevada City in 1855.
According to the inscription, "The marking of this lone grave
perpetuates the memory of the lone graves throughout the
state of California."
"Pioneer Grave," east of Nevada City, CA

Warren Saddler was one of those people who put
out his hand to catch a child's free-fall. He was one
of many heroic men who risked their lives and fortunes to pluck a soul from the edge of disaster.
Warren Saddler never set out to be a hero. He just
happened to meet a seven-year-old girl named
Emma at a place on the American River, not far
north of where James Marshall first caught the glint
of the gold that started it all.

It was spring, and the earth was beginning to
reveal treasures as waters washed over her surface.

Warren Saddler had settled down with his pan and rocker, looking for color in the black sand. His only companion was his pack mule. Ahead of the rush of 1849, Warren had staked a claim for himself at a place called Barne's Bar. He was looking forward to a golden season.

Emma Griffis and her wandering parents landed in a spot near Warren Saddler. In the beginning, Warren stuck to his own business of prospecting, even after shots were fired in the Griffis camp, and a "rough looking man" ended up dead. Even when the little girl was reported missing.

Warren wondered about the girl, where she might be. But mostly he was lonely, and as he moved around to find pay dirt, he thought of the home he had left behind.

> **Oh, how foolish I was to exchange home and comforts, where I had a good clean bed to lie down in, and plenty of friends, for a life in the lonely mountains. Where I was obliged to lie on the cold ground and eat any kind of provisions I could get to sustain life! It is certainly hard to think of.**

Warren may have been thinking of home and comforts when he happened on an Indian camp, hidden behind some chaparral. Curious, he crept up and watched the camp, noticing the surrounding trails.

> **Such blind trails leading from their camps, are retreat trails for their woman and children in time of trouble with other parties. There**

> trails always lead to some dark low
> hiding places to shelter them till the
> trouble is over, or in case of defeat,
> the Indians know where to find their
> families. In this way, they can escape
> from their enemies.

Idly watching the huts in the camp, suddenly he saw her—a little white girl. It was Emma. Warren could have left then, and no one would have known the difference. But, fighting his fear and masking his misgivings, he boldly approached the camp. He learned that Emma's kidnapper had left her there, and would return shortly.

Emma told him what had happened—how the partner of the man who was killed in their camp had promised to take her to the store and buy her "cakes and other nice things," but instead he kept on going into the woods. Warren asked if she wanted to go back to her parents. "Yes," she answered, "but I cannot find the way."

> This answer made my blood boil, also
> start the tears from my eyes, to think
> that poor little innocent child
> standing in front of me, was stolen
> from her mother and carried off
> hundreds of miles . . . by such a
> miserable wretch . . .. My feelings
> and sympathy for the poor child . . .
> caused me to say to myself this child
> is in need of protection by some one,
> and I will be that one, and take all
> the chances of loosing my life in
> getting possession of her.

And so Warren left with the girl—just ahead of the returning, drunken kidnapper, who was quickly dispatched after he attacked one of the Indians.

It was a loud beginning to a long journey to find Emma's parents. Spring had blossomed into summer, and Warren's thoughts of a golden season turned to his mission to deliver Emma safely to her parents. And so they set out on a long journey, she perched on his mule, he walking beside her, and lugging on his back all his belongings.

For nearly two months, the unlikely couple ricocheted from place to place. It was a crazy path on which Warren found Emma's parents and lost them again, and Emma was kidnapped again and rescued again.

Finally, they arrived at the place where the girl's parents were supposed to be waiting. At last, they thought, Emma was home. But her parents were nowhere to be found. They had gotten tired of waiting and were headed south for Stockton, they were told.

The exhausted little Emma, her hopes dashed, lay down and cried herself to sleep. "If I ever felt bad in my life it was while sitting and gazing on that sleeping disappointed child," Warren wrote. Before they were once more on their way, some miners took up a collection of gold for little Emma.

Warren and Emma trudged on, through rugged country and across three major rivers, where she was towed across, hanging onto the mule's tail "like a little lobster." Warren had grown fond of the girl, and no longer was lonely. He admired her grit. "Emma stood [the journey] like a lump of iron." She even kept calm when wolves surrounded them, and a grizzly bear came near.

Nearly three months after Emma last had seen her parents, she spotted a familiar sight—her cream-colored mule, who came trotting to meet her. As

Warren led the mule carrying Emma toward a tent, the girl's mother and father appeared. Reaching up to Emma, Warren set her down in front of her parents. "Here is your lost child," he announced.

After Warren had stayed for two days with the little family, the rescued Emma decided that now that she'd seen her parents, she wanted to go with Warren. "I don't want any body to take better care of me than you do," she told him.

Knowing the hard life of a miner, Warren convinced his little friend that she was better off now with her mother. And so, leaving behind the child who had brightened his life for much of what was to be his golden summer, Warren Saddler once more was on his way.

> **After I had the mules started, I**
> **looked around and saw her mother**
> **trying to wipe away the tears that**
> **was still streeming down her little**
> **cheeks, while her body was trembling**
> **looked to see me go and leave**
> **her. . . . I was soon out of sight . . ..**
> **Riding along alone, I began to think**
> **over the whole entire trip, from the**
> **first time we left the indian camp till**
> **we reached her mother's tent; which**
> **was a long teageous journey of**
> **hundreds of miles. I pushed along**
> **slowly till night and camped took**
> **care of my animals cooked my supper**
> **But there was no Emma to eat with**
> **me or look after. which made me feel**
> **lonely, although her little voice was**
> **still sounding in my ears. In the**
> **morning, I got an early start. My**
> **whole mind was bent for making**

**money to build up and make repairs
for the last time.**

For Warren Saddler, some of the golden summer
still remained.

KP 98

Emma's was just one of thousands of tales of
children caught up in the excitement, danger, dis-
ruption, and violence of the Gold Rush. Some lost
their innocence, even their lives, but others actually thrived on the experience.

Martha (Jennie) Ross Gentry was an eleven-year-
old forty-niner caught up in the whirl of the Gold
Rush. Her adventure began in Missouri, where she
was visiting her older sister whose husband had
been stricken with gold fever and planned to go and
take his wife along. Martha had heard stories of
"General" Sutter's little daughter finding many
nuggets of gold and begged her sister take her along
to California, where she could pick up nuggets too.

The tales, of course, stretched the truth. Johann
Sutter didn't even have a little girl. And, according
to some accounts, the children reported to have
found gold lying around at Sutter's Mill picked up
gold that had been placed there for them to find. But
no matter. Truth mattered little.

In just two weeks, the little group was ready to

leave, with no time even to say good-bye to Martha's mother, who lived two hundred and fifty miles away. Her mother received word by mail several weeks after her daughters had left. "But realizing that I was in safe hands, she calmly faced the inevitable," Martha wrote. As it turned out, Martha's brother, too, soon left for California, and caught up with Martha's party on the trail.

On the journey West, young Martha was fascinated by the Indians she encountered. She was one who held "the kindliest of feelings toward our red brothers" for the rest of her life, and was never afraid of them. She knew Indians at home, and wasn't afraid.

At a fort, "an old squaw" made her a pair of moccasins.

> **I distinctly recall the air of pride and dignity with which she came into our quarters, and seating herself with all the self-assurance of an honored guest, began to work upon the little moccasins. When they were completed, she gave them to me, and I wore them throughout the rest of my journey.**

Martha was appalled when her brother-in-law mocked some Indians. "[T]o me he seemed far below the Indian in breeding," and she worried that the Indians might retaliate for the insult. "I have often wondered," she wrote, "if much of the trouble between the Indians and white men was not caused by just such foolish and insulting actions."

In Placerville, the family made their little house of rough logs, with a stone fireplace and chimney— a home of luxury by most '49 standards. Young

Martha remembered beds made of "heaps of pine boughs. . . . A sweeter or more comfortabler resting place I have never found."

Children were rare in the mining camps, and many miners reached out to befriend and protect them. Luzena Wilson recalled miners passing around her babe in arms as though he were a small, wiggly treasure.

The miners showered Martha with attention. One of their games was challenging her to guess the weight of a nugget. If she guessed right, she got to keep it. She became expert at the game, and collected a fair fortune. The miners also would let children dig on their claims and keep what they found. With her first nugget, Martha bought a pair of shoes since the moccasins the "old squaw" had made for her had long since worn out.

Like most things on the carnival frontier, contentment did not last. In the spring, the family moved twice, and as her brother-in-law began building a canvas house, her sister, with whom she had shared so much, caught a fever. Neighbors and a doctor came to help, but no one could save her, and she died.

Suddenly, the young Martha was left "stranded and homeless" in the strange world of the Mother Lode. Who would take care of her? Where would she go? Her brother or brother-in-law would seem to have been the logical ones, but Martha made no mention of them.

She learned that "even the services of a child were much sought after, as I was soon to find out." And so Martha found work at a series of boarding houses. Her "mistress" stole the gold she had saved, and cheated her out of her most cherished possession—a silk shawl from China. Martha noticed that the woman also cheated her hotel patrons by "accidentally" spilling their gold dust and later mining it from underneath the floor boards.

As the girl moved from place to place, she watched with fascination as miners took big nuggets out of the earth—some bigger than a fist. She became a "fearless rider," encountered bears and panthers, and went to dances, where she "was always in demand as a partner."

Martha had been wandering the Mother Lode for a year and was becoming more free than a lady was supposed to be. "Older and wiser heads" decided it was time for Martha to go home to her mother. They collected money, gold dust, and two slugs (fifty dollar gold pieces) for her passage, and found a man to accompany her home.

Martha expressed no regret about leaving, but looked forward to another adventure—a trip home by ship, by way of Nicaragua. On the voyage to Nicaragua, Martha nearly fell off the ship when a rope she was swinging on careened over the water when the ship suddenly lurched, but she swung back to safety.

She did a thriving business on board hemming handkerchiefs. Fellow passengers presented to her a purse of money they had collected for her education, accompanied by a signed sheet that read, "Modesty and virtue adorn a lady." As she became more of a lady, she would be expected to adopt the modesty and virtue and stop having adventures.

But Martha was more of a lady than we would have thought at this point. When faced with riding a mule for part of the overland trip to the Caribbean, she balked.

> **I had always ridden on a side saddle, and my mule was not equipped with one. I must ride astride, and I shrank from the very thought, for in those days it was deemed highly improper for a woman or girl to use other than a side saddle. It took considerable persuasion to induce me to mount my beast, but at last I followed the example of the other ladies and our journey began.**

From there she finished her journey by steamer, farm wagon, stage, ferry, and horseback. As she rode the final distance home with her younger brother, cold reality began to hit her.

> **It was a cold, dismal winter day, and as I rode homeward, I looked at the snow covered ground and the bare limbs of the trees, and in spite of my eagerness to see my mother and sisters, I was homesick for the sunny land of California.**

It had been nearly two years since Martha had left home. Seeing her mother, she realized what a toll the time had taken, for "she had aged perceptibly in the interval." Martha learned that her brother had tried to reach her in California to accompany her home, but she already had left, so he decided to stay. The following winter, he contracted smallpox and died.

Of all her family that had gone to California, thirteen-year-old Martha alone returned.

Her mother, still grieving for her lost children, put away Martha's precious mementos of her California adventures. And, like so many California dreams, they went up in smoke, burned with her mother's house during the Civil War.

But the dream stayed with Martha, and twenty-five years later, she took a train back to California, where she stayed.

Mrs. Lee Whipple-Haslam remembered in later years her adventures on the carnival frontier near Sonoma, in the southern mines. The girl whose father called her Tom trekked to California with her parents in 1852—the year the westward trails were the most crowded.

Like Martha Ross, "Tom" held a vivid memory of Indian people they met, and of some Indian moccasins. At an Indian village, she spotted a pair of beaded Indian moccasins she longed to own. On impulse, she grabbed them, and took off toward camp, with Indians in hot pursuit. It was her father who caught her, returned the moccasins, and gave her a humiliating spanking.

By the time her family reached Placerville, the "alkali and dust had done for my eyes, and I was nearly blind." In time, Tom recovered. They went on to Shaws Flat, near Sonora, and moved into a log cabin with a dirt floor and canvas roof. There, her mother planted the morning glory seeds she had brought from Missouri. The morning glory would grow to cover the walls.

One day soon after their arrival, her mother opened a small trunk that had survived the journey. Tom watched, wide-eyed, as her mother uncovered fresh dresses—one for herself and one for her daughter. And there was something else. There in the trunk was a pair of beautiful beaded moccasins—the ones that had prompted her spanking. Back there on the plains, Tom's father had traded for the moccasins she had stolen, and tucked them away for her.

Like Martha Ross, Tom was favored by the miners, who called her Tom, or Little Sister, Miss Pike, Missouri, or Frank's girl. The miners taught the girl woodcraft, how to use a compass by reading rocks and trees, and how to use firearms. "Old as I am," she boasted many years later, "[I] could take the head off of a gray squirrel in the tallest pine . . .."

She remembered a childhood living among honest miners, gamblers, hurdy-gurdy girls, Chinese, Irish, Indians, Mexicans, and Frenchmen. Among her pleasant childhood memories was the food she could buy in the store.

I remember the first dried apples that appeared in the stores; they were small, sour, cut in quarters strung on twine and sold for three dollars a yard. Then a few bottles of pickles appeared—quarts and pints. They sold for $5 a quart and $2.50 a pint. The bottles, to my inexperienced eyes, were marvels of beauty, green, pink and clear glass. The boys gave me many of the bottles . . .. Some of the happiest memories of my childhood are associated with those pickle bottles.

After two years, the family moved farther into the wilderness, where they lived happily and sufficiently. But they were not far enough away from trouble, and the next year the rose-colored world of Tom's childhood came to a mean end when her father was shot and killed. In their grief, the girl and her mother and, by then, little brother received protection.

The miners—God bless them—threw a cordon of protection around that humble but desolate home, and none of the rough element ever dared to intrude or molest the helpless and sorrowing inmates.

Following the pattern of many women of the Mother Lode, Tom's mother opened a boarding house for the growing population of the camp to support her little family.

The girl seemed to sympathize with the nearby Indian people the settlers called "Diggers." She acknowledged that "[b]efore the advent of the white man, the Indians lived a peaceful, happy life, with the exception of occasional trouble with [other Indians]."

Yet in her old age, Mrs. Lee Whipple-Haslam concluded that "We were instruments known and recognized as Pioneers, and predestined to civilize the Pacific Coast."

Seven-year-old Benjamin Bonney, who came to the Mother Lode before the Gold Rush, had vivid memories of his 1845 overland trek. He remembered crossing a sage brush desert where the sage tore into the oxen's legs. The spines of the prickly pear cactus penetrated their hooves and cut the feet of the children, who by then were walking barefoot.

His young eyes watched fellow travelers' ugly attacks on lone Indians. He remembered his mother placing a dying Indian on her quilt and offering him a drink.

When his party reached the land that soon would be gold rush country, the ragged travelers camped by a mountain stream for three days "to rest the teams and let the women wash the clothing and get things fixed up." It was a fine October day and the water ran low. On a gravel bar, he picked up some particles that the company's doctor diagnosed as pure gold. But Ben's father dismissed the doctor's diagnosis, calling him a visionary.

Ben and the doctor picked up all the gold they could find and talked about coming back to this place in the spring. But the doctor died at Sutter's Fort a few months later. The next year, the Mexican government ordered emigrants either to leave or become Mexican citizens. Ben's family left and headed north to Oregon.

After Marshall's gold discovery in 1848, Ben's uncle returned to the place where the boy had found the gold. It "had already been staked out, and proved to be very rich ground." Ben himself never returned to that spot.

Young Hermann Sharmann's story is something of a mining camp "Gift of the Magi." After a terrible overland journey in 1849, Hermann's family settled on an isolated gold claim. Canvas was the little family's only shelter, the earth their only bed. Both parents lay ill, the father with scurvy.

With Christmas approaching, Hermann and his brother took the ten dollars worth of gold dust they had saved and rode ninety miles byhorseback to Marysville to bring back Christmas. They returned with a tree—a branch of pine—and the most treasured gift they could think of—food.

Proudly, the boys prepared their grand meal of

flapjacks, biscuits, coffee, and a precious can of peaches. Then, in a grand procession, they brought in their prized gifts to lay before their parents.

> **And then we had our crushing disappointment. Neither of them could touch the delicacy. Nor could either taste the meal which we had arranged with so much pride. We both cried a little, but our mother comforted us and told us that we should eat the share for them.**

Hermann never forgot their "sad celebration under the canvas roof on the banks of the Upper Feather River."[2]

Indian and Spanish-speaking children helped their families mine in the months between the gold discovery and the Gold Rush. Fewer children were in the diggings as the Mother Lode became virtually male territory.

But children's fascination for gold kept them hanging around the gold fields, sometimes helping, sometimes finding their own, sometimes just watching. And they saw what the miners did with it.

> **The miners had so much gold they didn't know what to do with it. They dug holes in the floor and buried it under the rugs. . . . To this day I know very well where there is plenty of fine ground full of gold. That is another story.**
> —Sarrah Willits Berry, 1853

Dangers lurked in the gold fields and on the way there, especially for children, who often had to take responsibilities expected of adults. Imagine the terror felt by teen Charles True, who had to swim a horse across the angry Platte River to find feed on the other side. "There was nothing to do but to obey orders," he remembered, and "no way to shirk the dangerous duty."

In 1845, another teenager, Moses Schallenberger, volunteered to stay behind at Truckee Lake (now Donner Lake) to guard his family's belongings while others went on ahead to Sutter's Fort for help. The boy was trapped in the snow for nearly three months before his rescue.

The next year, the tragic troupe of travelers known as the Donner Party were trapped in the same area where young Moses spent the winter, and some used the cabin he had built.

Young Virginia Reed, a member of the Donner Party, had seen her father banished from the wagon train. Seeing her mother's distress, at that moment she became a woman.

> [W]ith the little ones clinging around
> her and no arm to lean upon, it
> seemed suddenly to make a woman of
> me. I realized that I must be strong
> and help mama bear her sorrows.

When the last rescue party left the place of the Donner party's entrapment, Tamsen Donner chose to stay and die with her dying husband instead of accompanying her children to Sutter's Fort and safety. After their rescue, three barefooted girls wandered among the canvas houses of Sutter's Fort, reciting to strangers what their mother had taught them to say: "We are the children of Mr. and Mrs. George Donner." And they added, "And our parents are dead." The children were taken in by people at the fort, including some members of the Donner Party.

Once children reached California, they were hardly safe from danger.

"This is an awful place for children," wrote Dame Shirley. She often saw children run to the very edge of a coyote hole—"many of them sixty feet in depth—which have been excavated in the hope of finding gold, and of course left open."

The moral dangers were nearly as lethal as the physical ones. Children watched as the carnival parade of gamblers, prostitutes, and other "moving microbes" passed before them.

Boys routinely prowled the gambling houses, trading in their gold, and mimicking the behavior they saw.

> **The children participate in all the vices of their elders. I saw boys, from six upward, swaggering through the streets, begirt with scarlet sash, in exuberant collar and bosom, segar in mouth, uttering huge oaths, and occasionally treating men and boys at the bars.**
>
> —Eliza Farnham

Mrs. D.B. Bates figured that of two hundred women in a mining town, three or four might be "pure, high-minded, and virtuous." No doubt her standards were impossibly high. But prostitutes proliferated, and young girls—and boys—noticed that most of them wore finer clothes and lived in nicer houses than their mothers did—hardly a selling point for purity and virtue.

Mrs. Bates told the sad story of fifteen-year-old Lillie, who, despite the frantic efforts of her mother, fell victim to the allures of the fast life. Lillie could be seen "mounted on a glossy, lithe limbed race-horse," her riding outfit "ornamented with a hundred and fifty gold buttons . . .."

"Gold and diamonds were showered" upon the poor thing, and "the hilarity of despair seemed to have fast possession of her." She got mixed up with a married gambler, and presumably went downhill from there.

Perhaps the most poignant stories are of the children we hardly see through the fogged lenses of history. We see only glimpses of the Indian boys and girls stolen and used as servants and prostitutes. The black girls and boys not allowed to attend schools reserved for whites.

According to author Curt Gentry, more than half of Peruvian prostitutes in San Francisco in 1848 and 1849 were still in their teens, some as young as thirteen.

Many Chinese prostitutes, too, were just children. Mrs. D.B. Bates told of a young Chinese man named "John" who rescued a sixteen-year-old girl whose "owner" was beating her. The assailant gathered thirty companions and came after John, who with the girl had taken refuge in a hotel. There John learned that the only way he could prevent the girl from being returned to her savage owner was to marry her—right there and then. And so he did. We can assume it was a happier arrangement for the girl than what she had before.

In the best of all worlds, a child would be regarded as a little person who brings out the best of human intentions and potential, someone to be protected and cherished. Ideally, it would have been that way in the Mother Lode. Realistically, too many children and adults were not protected and cherished.

However, for many who came to the Mother Lode, like Warren Saddler and the Chinese man known as John, children did bring out the nobility that lies in the souls of all humanity.

CHAPTER NINE

To Make Good Bread

**To make good bread and to
understand the process of making it
is the duty of every woman, indeed
an art that should never be neglected
in the education of a lady. The lady
derives her title from 'dividing or
distributing bread'; the more perfect
the bread the more perfect the lady.**

—Sarah Josepha Hale,
Receipts for the Millions, 1857

After the first burst of carnival fandango,
women—or more specifically, ladies—began to
arrive, determined to slow things down to a cultured waltz. The ladies came to tend to housekeep-
ing—at home and in the community. They came to
tame.

And the ladies made bread. Sarah Josepha Hale,
educator of many nineteenth century ladies as
editor of *Godey's Ladies Book,* was right about the
title of lady. The ancient meaning of the word is
"Giver of Bread." In the old matriarchal societies,
women controlled the making, storage, and distrib-
ution of bread—the main source of food, and the
main currency. It was the women who were the
community power and money brokers, like the

Indian women of the Mother Lode. But the ladies called them squaws.

The miners looked to the ladies to civilize what quickly had become a mad world. They looked to the ladies to make things clean, to symbolize the home left behind. To be perfect. To bake bread—not hard tack, not duff, not johnny cakes. Bread from dough, lovingly kneaded. Bread that rises magically to a puffy softness. Home-baked bread that teases the nostrils as it bakes, bread that melts butter when it's hot, bread that nourishes the body and warms the soul.

Things got desperate for the miners with no women around. When one showed up, you'd think an angel had fluttered down from the sky. "The few present wore an Aphrodite girdle, which shed a glamour over imperfections," wrote the venerable historian Hubert H. Bancroft, "till they found themselves divinities, centres of chivalric adorers."

Many men carried on about how they needed women—Aphroditic girdles and all—to nurture them, to clean up their messes, and to calm down all those other degenerate men out there.

For the first two years, or up to the arrival of the emigration from across the plains in the fall of '50, the condition of the mining population, especially their carelessness in

> regard to appearances, mode of life,
> and habits in general, showed
> conclusively that man, when alone,
> and deprived of that influence which
> the presence of woman only can
> produce, would in a short time
> degenerate into a savage and
> barbarous state.[1]

Certainly not all men wanted women around. Belgian miner Jean-Nicholas Perlot described a simple, "rude and miserable life" that was "comparatively happy; we knew only one passion, that for gold; on the physical side, we felt only one need, to eat; it was our principal and, very often, our sole preoccupation." At the end of the day, the miners would sing of their happiness while accompanying themselves on violin, flute, accordion, or cornet.

But one day in 1855 the inevitable happened. A woman entered the camp. "Eve or Pandora! She brought them ineffable joys and exquisite sorrows, the latter, I think, in a greater proportion," grumbled Jean-Nicholas. From that moment, everything changed—no more peaceful life, concerts, or songs. Where some blamed chaos on the absence of women, Jean-Nicholas blamed this woman for spoiling his perfectly happy, "miserable life."[2]

Despite spoil-sports like Jean-Nicholas, most ladies took seriously their duty to come to men's rescue.

> Come to the country which is the
> home of those you are bound to
> adhere to and save, when they are
> ready to receive you. Come strong in

"At Last—the Sonora Emigrant Trail, 1853"

Emigrant woman carrying baby and collecting wood while crossing the Sonora emigrant trail on the last stretch to California.

Courtesy Tuolumne Museum and History Center, Sonora, CA

Photo by Lynn Jerome

the resolution to be true to yourselves and to them, under all trials; to put away pining and discontent, and face your hardest fortune bravely . . ..

—Eliza Farnham

In case a woman didn't think she had enough advice and rules on how to perform her duties, how to behave, and how to dress, from ladies' magazines, preachers, husbands, fathers, and other experts, she could get herself a copy of "Commandments for California Wives."

This document was a spoof on "The Miners' Ten Commandments," which was a spoof on miners' codes of conduct. Basically, the Miners' Commandments admonished men to behave themselves—to stay on their own claims, refrain from gambling and getting drunk, and honor Sunday by doing proper work:

> **yet thou washest all thy dirty shirts, darnest all thy stockings, tap thy boots, mend thy clothing, chop thy whole week's firewood, make up and bake thy bread and boil thy pork and beans, that thou wait not when thou returnest from thy long-tom weary.**
> —from California Letter Sheets

Also, the miners shall not kill anybody, nor even worse—steal anything. For that, the penalty was severe—hanging, lashing, head shaving, or branding. They shall not lie, nor "commit unsuitable matrimony," nor "covet thy neighbor's wife." And finally, they shall return home.

Tellingly, "The Miners' Ten Commandments" said nothing about visiting prostitutes.

The "Commandments for California Wives" may have been a spoof, but they embodied ancient codes of conduct for "True Women" from Biblical times and before. These Commandments instructed wives to be thrifty, to avoid being smarter than their husbands, not to drag their skirts in the mud, to be faithful, work hard, smile, be pretty and cheerful, and most importantly—*keep quiet and don't complain.*

Oh yes, and read twice a week the last chapter of

Proverbs and the fifth chapter of Ephesians. Key verses in those two Bible readings are, "Let him drink, and forget his poverty, and remember his misery no more," and "Wives, submit yourselves unto your own husbands, as unto the Lord."

For all you wives who just curled your lip at this last verse, read on:

> **Thou shalt not give these commandments a revengeful interpretation; nor curl thy lip in insulted contempt, nor flash fire from the corners of thine eyes.**

Finally, unmarried ladies, as well as married ones, shall come to California when called.

"AMEN—So mote it be."

Whatever that means.

And so they came. Among them were three young ladies who left "civilization" behind to sail to the land of gold. Two were young wives and one a single school teacher who soon would marry. All found that their presence alone was not enough to tame this country. That would take some time, and some action.

Twenty-three-year-old Clementine Brainard honestly tried to abide by the Commandments to California Wives (except for the Bible verse about letting him drink). Young Clementine recorded two years of her life in Columbia, one of the first towns of the southern districts to settle down.

By 1853, Columbia had mushroomed from a mining camp of tents and brush huts to a busy, commercial town with real streets and two churches. One of the richest towns in the Mother Lode, it now had more than one-hundred businesses, banks and markets, along with saloons and fandango houses. There were nearly one-hundred families, and nearly ten times that many bachelors. And hundreds of "Red Light" women.

Miners swarmed in and out of the town, depending on the weather and availability of water and, of course, gold. There were the usual murders, duels, robberies, and fights between miners and gamblers, between miners and the water company, between "white" miners and "foreigners," and between any men who got in each other's way.

Enter Clementine. A lady, one of several wives from Maine. A lady who had left a loving family, friends, a nice home, and a place in the community to come to this place that obviously needed ladies like her.

Think how different her arrival in 1853 Columbia must have been from Luzena Wilson's first sight of Deer Creek Diggins in 1850. Luzena arrived in the calm before the storm, and saw the coming of the carnival frontier. Clementine was part of the attempt to slow it down.

Luzena, like Clementine, was a lady, married, with two children. Luzena wore proper calico dresses, but probably shorter than was proper, and without the yards of ladylike petticoats, in order to maneuver in the camp mud. Luzena had tramped over the California Trail, where she had gotten broken in on how crude life could be. She earned her own money, knew how to live in a tent, and had little time for anything but work. Few other women were there to look over her shoulder and monitor her behavior as a lady.

Clementine, on the other hand, depended on the earnings of her merchant husband, who frequently was gone to San Francisco. She lived in relative isolation, and brooded over her own faults, which she was convinced were many. And she felt the eyes of the other ladies on her, measuring her manner of dress and behavior as a lady.

The young wife felt the weight of her religion, a constant reminder of her duty to be pious and useful. If only she could be perfect, she could help to bring order to this place, "to cast my influence in favor of religion, temperance, and good morals . . . ." And when she did something evil, such as sleeping late on the Sabbath, she knew her failure "must be all my fault for God never forsakes us."

With her merchant husband often away, loneliness was Clementine's frequent and unwelcome companion. Thoughts of home back in Maine frequently came flooding in—of pleasant times with her mother and sister, of younger days in school, jovial times at Thanksgiving, and sleigh-rides in December.

But no matter how lonely or sad she might be, Clementine always knew that she was better off than other women around her.

At the rich diggings on Gold Hill, she "saw how miners wives have to live," and felt sorry for a woman who lived in a cabin there.

With her friends, she visited the "Diggers" in their "wigwams." She pitied this "race of human beings so degraded as these. . . . If there is anything we have reason to thank God for it is that we had our birth and being in an enlightened land: and had Christian parents to instruct us."

"Emma" from Railroad Flat
Courtesy Calaveras County Historical Society, San Andreas, CA

Clementine also noted the miners' chronic water shortages, and ongoing efforts to divert water from area rivers and streams into the dry diggings. Perhaps she didn't realize that taking the "Digger" Indians' water away served to "degrade" their way of life.

On the first day of May, if the weather was fine and the hillsides not too muddy, Clementine would go "Maying." She would search the hillside for spring flowers to put in little baskets and leave for special friends. One May Day, she found "a beautiful May basket hung at our door this morning—Mrs. Bridges has gone off a Maying . . .."

Columbia remained a difficult place for a lady. And as more ladies came to the country, it became important to separate themselves and their families from "bad influences."

Clementine declined to see off an acquaintance who was leaving town.

> [D]id not think is best as I had
> heared considerable against her
> character of late, think she is a
> person that the least one has to do
> with her the better it is for them.

And she carefully screened social invitations to parties and balls because "some are invited that are not fit for decent people to associate with."

Violence was a reality Clementine could not ignore. One day a mob stampeded past her house in pursuit of a man the mobsters were intent on hanging.

> It really seemed that we're living in
> Cal. in '49 and the Lynch Law was
> the only one that prevailed. Oh! May

**we soon have such laws here as we
have at home; and may they be
enforced.**

Clementine helped organize activities to benefit
schools, churches, and fraternal organizations. She
applauded a woman-led move to observe Sunday
store closings so the Sabbath would be observed
righteously, "and then we may hope for a reforma-
tion in Columbia."

She signed the temperance pledge and believed
that with others signing it, "there is a brighter time
coming for the society of Columbia." She was
pleased to attend a party where no liquor was
served.

**[It was] sayed to be the first party in
Columbia where they had no
liquors—think this is a proof that . . .
a party could have been got up in a
mining town in Cal. in so good style.**

Though she strived for a stable home and community, Clementine's own life was not settled. For a
time, she took in a series of boarders. In 1854, an
arsonist's fire burned up most of Columbia, including the Brainards' house and store. Months later, a
fierce wind blew down their house frame.

Soon after the couple moved into a new home, a
baby—Charlie—appeared. Clementine never mentioned a birth, but perhaps the clue was her entry
that she "had a nice 'Christmas present'" in 1854.

Clementine's journal ended nearly a year later,
after noting more deaths, another murder, and a new
"burying ground" in town. Her husband, Marcellus,
died of malaria in 1856, and she returned home to
Maine, where she remarried.

In 1855, the last year of Clementine Brainard's journal, a twenty-year-old single woman arrived in Columbia from Vermont. Ellen Sears came to join her father and sister, who earlier had come to Columbia. They soon would be joined by Ellen's mother and brothers.

Ellen lived in her father's house and, like many other ladies who came to the Mother Lode, took her meals at a boarding house. She shed some light on what houses in 1855 Columbia looked like:

> **Houses were flimsy affairs, cloth and paper partitions, still they seemed very snug, and neat after the great rambling houses in the East. They were mostly painted white, if at all, and had green shutters.**

Ellen came to teach school, which she began in a private one-room school a week after her arrival.

> **The school house contained one rather large room. There were from sixteen to twenty pupils, each of whom brought me, weekly, a Mexican silver dollar. Some of my pupils were larger than I, but most were children anywhere from four to fourteen years.**

Ellen lived on "Gold Hill," where Clementine Brainard would take walks and visit the diggings and cabins. It's also where the two churches were located. Ellen described how the miners lived.

> **Higher up, the hill was all dotted over with miners' cabins. They built themselves small shacks and staked out their claims. Here they kept house for themselves, living mostly on pork and beans and soda biscuit. Sometimes they gave little parties and invited in a few friends. At such times they made heroic attempts to have everything spick and span, but most of the men were not great successes at housekeeping.**

After school, Ellen wrote, boys often "cradled out a dollar or two from the bed of the creek . . . ." She noted that as the "only unmarried young lady," she was in great demand at the dances they would have in new houses "before the partitions were put up."

> **A country girl, writing to her friends, says of the polka, that 'the dancing does not amount to much, but the hugging is heavenly.'**
> —Mariposa *Gazette*

Like Clementine, Ellen carefully noted the distinction between the "ladies" and the "other" women. Besides "about twenty-five women" in town,

> **there were about 300 women of the 'Gold Belt' (the badge of the 'Red**

Light' women). Their quarters were elaborately furnished and looked attractive from the outside, but the women themselves were a dowdy, dirty, run-down looking lot.

When a "woman of refinement and character" came into a store, Ellen noted, the "Red Light" women would stand back and allow the lady to make her purchase first.

Ellen poignantly described a town still in the throes of carnival, still beyond taming by the few "ladies" present.

I have often thought had conditions been more settled something might have been done for these poor unhappy women, but everything was on the move. Today they were here, tomorrow no one knew where these derelicts of society went. Men were rich today, flush and confident; perhaps the next they went back home broken in health and pocket, or cast out with those women who fell into the great human scrap heap, unfit to go back to their homes. No one expected to remain in California;

**it was 'make your pile' then home—
home—home! This was the slogan.
Few had any idea of other
possibilities of money making than
mining.**

As testimony to the craziness of the times, Ellen
told a tale of horror. It was one of the most notorious incidents in Columbia's wild history: the hanging of John Barclay from the town's water flume in
October 1855. Like much of the violence in the
Mother Lode, Barclay's fate got tangled up in issues
of race and class.

John Barclay shot and killed Jack Smith, after
Jack got into a drunken fight with John's wife (some
say lover), Martha Carlos. She was a Spanish-speaking woman who ran "Martha's Saloon," known also
as a brothel. Jack was a popular man with a good
reputation. John had a bad reputation mainly
because of his association with Martha and the
saloon.

When the miners heard about the shooting, a
mob stormed the jail where John was being held and
dragged him out, past Ellen Sears' house.

**As this mob of 2,000 or more people
came roaring up the streets they
levelled the fences on both sides of
the street. At the rear were 200 or
more 'Red Light' women, cursing and
screaming vengeance on those who
would put one of their friends to
death. Here right in sight of our
house they hung Barkley [sic],
refusing to cut him down until the
next day so that all might see his
fate. . . . In the morning Barkley's**

**body was taken down and he was
buried before Jack Smith.**

The Presbyterian minister, Mr. Brodt, showed up at Ellen's door to comfort her. Soon the two were married, returned to the East coast, and eventually had nine children.

Emily Lindsey Rolfe was twenty-two when she arrived in Nevada City from Massachusetts in 1854 with her new husband, who had first trekked to the Mother Lode three years before.

Emily was not impressed when she first saw the house her husband had prepared for her: "The view was not artistic."

The house, unevenly constructed of wood, had been freshly painted and papered in an attempt to hide some sins. Grease spots had soaked through the paper, and

**I noticed two little pyramids shaped
like blocks on top of the paste boards
below the grease spots on the paper. I
investigated and found the cold
grease that had piled up from fry
pans that had evidently been hung up
by the miners without having been
washed. The grease had drained from
the pans and the painter had painted
over them.**

Pigs slept under the house, and their attendant fleas kept Emily awake for most of her first night in the house. When she told her husband the pigs would have to go, he informed her that they were "healthy as they ate the refuse that was thrown from the house." The refuse would have to go too, she insisted.

He sent a colored man the next day
and the miscellaneous things that
came to light were astonishing to a
person just from civilization. There
were gum boots, old coats, pants, and
vest, red shirts, blue shirts, and white
ones, any number of old socks,
bottles of all sizes and description,
tin cans of every shape and size,
bones that the dogs had carried under
there and I cannot describe the odor
or now remember the number of
wheel barrow loads that were
dumped into Deer Creek.

The house itself had an intriguing movement to it.

Our house was lined with cloth and
when a gust of wind came . . . it
would sail up and down. I imagined
myself on ship board and felt sea
sick.

Emily observed with amusement the dress of Nevada City's "newly made rich." At a wedding where all the "respectable" ladies wore their best dresses, one lady came laden with gold: a gold comb in her hair, gold chain at her neck with a gold watch attached, two gold brooches, gold belt buckle, and gold bracelets on each wrist. She told Emily later that her husband had given her the gold jewelry, and wanted her to wear it all "to show his generosity to his wife."

A few years after her arrival, Emily was watching an encounter between her husband and two men over a building lot. As the men approached her husband, one of them knocked Emily's husband, "Mr. R.," to the ground and was pounding on him.

Emily screamed, picked up a rock, and ran over and grabbed the man's hair and hit him twice with the rock. By the time the other man could pull Emily off his companion, and pull him off Mr. R., the injured attacker had sustained a wound requiring three stitches.

> **A crowd had collected and a friend suggested I go to the house and he went with me as Mr. J. and Mr. R. had to have a word fight. On the way to the house we picked up my petticoat, which had fallen off when I fell down.**

Two months after fighting off her husband's attacker, Emily Rolfe bore her first baby.

Emily was one of many women who took direct action when warranted. In San Andreas, in the southern mines, a woman caught an unfortunate would-be chicken thief.

CRIME WAVE
HITS MINING CAMPS

CAMP SECO, JAN. 20, 1858.—Poverty Bar, Campo Seco, Winters' Bar and vicinity are infested with a set of petty thieves. Robbing hen-roosts, milking cows, stealing calf-skins, picks and shovels, etc. is the order of the day. A few nights ago an attempt was being made to rob the hen-roost of Mr. O'Hara. Mrs. O'Hara, hearing the disturbance, rushed out and met the thief with chickens in hand. Collaring the marauder, Mrs. O'Hara screamed for her daughter to bring a pistol and light. Unable to loosen the grip of Mrs. O'Hara, the man succeeded in squirming out of the coat and vanished before the daughter arrived with light and pistol. However, Mrs. O'Hara saved her chickens and still has the man's coat.

—San Andreas *Independent*

The editor of the Mariposa *Gazette,* a known misogynist, received a momento of his run-in with the town mothers after he wrote an article brandishing his distaste for children. The fed-up women one day marched into his shop, helped themselves to an apronful of metal type, and took it to a foundryman. They commissioned him to cast a caricature of the grump with the inscription "To the illustrious editor of the Gazette from the mothers of Mariposa for the interest and affection manifest in their children."[3]

Like the ladies of Mariposa, ladies throughout the Mother Lode were getting louder and more assertive in their charge to clean things up—in their communities as well as in their homes.

What the women in mind meant that many of the men would have to change. They'd have to clean themselves up, stay sober, watch their language, stop gambling, and make room for women in their laws. But that wasn't what a lot of the men had in mind. As in the Commandments for California Wives, they wanted the women to be pretty and helpful, not to spoil their fun. Whatever happened to the part about silence and submission?

Women discovered they couldn't tame the country by remaining silent. Therein lay the seeds of thorny issues still being debated in California, and all over the world.

The women became bolder. In Columbia, women like Clementine Brainard and Ellen Sears were instrumental in funding and establishing schools, churches, libraries, literary and music societies. Ladies held calico parties to raise money for families of miners injured or killed in their work. They took on issues of drunkenness, mob violence, and prostitution.

In Columbia, after several disastrous fires, ladies took action on fire control, which everyone wanted, but few wanted to pay for. "It was up [to] the women of Columbia to get things moving as usual," according to one writer. "[T]hey had to face the ridicule and in some cases, even the opposition of the men."[4]

The women put on a Fire Engine Festival and took paid subscriptions for fire protection. Within a few weeks, they had raised almost two thousand dollars. Some of the money was used to bring "Papeete," a used fire engine from Brooklyn, New York.

Women—many of them from New York—began to come into the Mother Lode, lecturing on temperance, morality, women's rights. Eliza Farnham was one of these "strong-minded females." Sarah Pellet, famous for her lecturing on temperance while wearing brown bloomers, was another. She inspired this reaction from one newspaper writer:

> [S]everal ladies, remarkable for their masculine tendencies and for the total absence of those more refined attributes [read *silence*] which lend to the female character its greatest charms, have come among us from the great hotbed of transcendentalism at the East—each bent on engrafting upon the tender stock of California her peculiar view of everything connected with our human economy.[5]

Many of the "strong-minded women" who came from "the great hotbed of transcendentalism at the East" were connected with the Transcendentalist circle of Emerson, Thoreau, Margaret Fuller, and others. Many were Spiritualists who, like Jeanne d'Arc, believed in direct revelation rather than receiving Truth through men in authority.

Nevada City and Grass Valley women were

among the first California women to organize for the right to vote. Emily Rolfe, the one who fought off her husband's attacker with a rock, was one of them.

With statehood in 1850 and in the first few years afterward, California women won some rights women in most other states didn't have. As the state began to organize, a sort of what-the-hell atmosphere prevailed. You might as well try different ways of doing things, because if it didn't work, you could always go back and change it later. Which they did, as we shall see.

The new California government didn't invent the rights it granted to married women early on. Married Spanish and Mexican women already had rights of property and ownership before the Anglos took over. Their laws were based on protecting the rights of the family, not just the man, as in Anglo law. American law was based on old English common law, which decreed that in marriage a woman and man become one person, and that is the man. The wife disappears before the law.

Based on old Spanish and Mexican laws, American women in California were granted rights to carry on their own businesses in their own names as "sole traders." They also had rights to divorce, and to own their own property, though husbands had control over the wife's property. Still, the early laws were better for women in California were better than in any other state, at least for a while.

And so, as more women came into the Mother Lode, some used California's legal freedoms for their own benefit.

If her husband wasn't treating her right, or if the gold gleamed brighter on the other side of town, a woman could get a divorce.

Forty-niner Lucy Stoddard Wakefield decided to

divorce her abusive husband while on the trail. In California, she got her divorce and made her way to Placerville. There, free from her husband's demands, she started a lucrative pie-baking business and built an independent life. A male admirer could figure only one explanation for her success:

> **[H]er talents appear to me of A**
> **higher order than I supposed them to**
> **be . . . Her head is Masculine rather**
> **than Feminine.**[6]

Dame Shirley took advantage of the divorce law and left her doctor husband, and Eliza Farnham left her abusive husband as well. Some women flitted from one man to the next, and probably a lot more thought about it than did it.

> **[I]t is all the go here for Ladys to**
> **leave there Husbands two out of three**
> **do it**
>
> —Abby Mansur, 1853

In one day alone in 1851, a Nevada City judge had "10 divorce cases on hand to dispose of in one day." All plaintiffs were women, most charging "extreme cruelty." Accompanying one woman was "her new friend who was engaged to marry her as soon as she could get the old one off." Also on the docket for that day were ten weddings.

Ideally, if her husband earned enough, a lady shouldn't have to work. Dame Shirley was one whose husband earned the living, and she boarded out and hired her washing done.

But many middle class women made use of the "sole trader" laws, and made and kept their own money. In the Gold Rush years, sole traders were most likely to run boarding houses, but they also ran stores, restaurants, and hotels. Many women were community medicine women, though they weren't paid what they were worth, if anything.

Doña Martinez, a wealthy woman from Baja California, traveled to the gold country by horseback. She employed her entourage on a mining claim, made a nice pile, and had a town named after her. Other Hispanic women ran dance halls, cafes, and stores, and some were opera singers, belly dancers, and bullfighters.[7]

> **A genuine Gipsey woman, whose name we have not learned, is now doing things for the anxious in Hornitos, and will soon be here, where she will, for the trifle of $5, tell one all he ever knew or heard of—all he ever expects to do, can do, or will do, and much that he might like to do. Young folks in love, and old ones in expectation, can be informed as to what will be, by just handing over $5.**
>
> —Mariposa *Gazette*

Black women were among those who rushed to the Mother Lode. Some came to California as slaves, like Biddy Mason, who drove livestock across the plains while caring for her three small children. California was a free state, largely because white miners didn't want slaves working in the mines, making their own work look like "slave labor." Though slavery technically was illegal, some owners still could keep their slaves if they had brought them into California themselves.

Some black people came to the country free, and

**Monroe Family,
Coloma, CA**
*Courtesy Marshall Gold
Discovery State Historic
Park, Coloma, CA*

**A memorial marks the
Monroe family homesite
at Marshall Gold
Discovery State Historic
Park, Coloma, CA**

some won their freedom after they arrived. But California also had a fugitive slave law, and until 1863, black people could not testify in court, even on their own behalf.

In the early Gold Rush years, the Mother Lode was a sanctuary of sorts for black people. Black miners were not unusual, though they had to be careful not to flaunt any success they had.

Laws and tradition discriminated against both women and minorities, and black women were expected to take the lowest-paid, most menial jobs. Because black children were not accepted in community schools, some black women started and taught in private schools. And they were entrepreneurs and civic leaders, laying foundations for their families and communities.

By 1855, the nearly five thousand black people in California owned property assessed at two million four hundred thousand dollars. Some of those property owners were women. Biddy Mason, for example, won her freedom, saved and invested the money she earned as a nurse in Los Angeles, and became a wealthy philanthropist and community leader.

Nancy Gooch traveled the overland trail as a slave in 1849 to Coloma, where James Marshall found that first gold. Nancy won her freedom with statehood in 1850, and went on to "make her pile" by doing laundry and other chores for the miners. Later, Nancy bought the freedom of her son and his wife, Andrew and Sara Ellen Monroe, who traveled from Missouri to join her. Eventually, the family acquired eighty acres of land, including the place where Marshall found his gold.

In the early mining frontiers, most women were neither upper nor middle class, and many were "foreigners." Most available work involved some kind of service to the men—prostitution, entertainment, cooking, washing, and cleaning.

In reality, there was no well-paid, secure work on the mining frontier. A mining camp could grow overnight into a boom town, bust tomorrow, and be empty next week. A woman could be making a lot of dough selling pies one day, and the miners could be off for Some Place Else next week.

Women couldn't count on laws continuing to protect them. According to authors Joan Jensen and Gloria Ricci Lothrop, women lost many of the rights they won with statehood. Newer laws tightened control of husbands over wives' property, and limited sole trader rights.

> **By the end of the century, California women had no more rights than did women in most of the eastern states. Not until after California women obtained the vote in 1911 were married women able to regain their property rights.[8]**

The winning, then losing, of rights fits the historical pattern described by author Marilyn French, and experienced by women around the world.

> **First, women gain the use of power— not the right to it—in periods of loose control. In conditions of severe hardship, . . . women and men struggle together for survival; in periods of tight control, men exclude women.[9]**

The women of California and throughout the West would win rights, only to see them lost as they

gained too much power and became too uppity—
especially on the issue of alcohol. Believing drunkenness to be the root of most of the evils they saw,
many women went against the commandment to
heed the Bible verse that says "Let him drink," and
made public their fight against drinking. As lawmakers and enforcers became more protective of
their rights to drink, they tightened legal control of
women's lives.

The women didn't give up, and ultimately won
back property rights and then voting rights, in a
seamless struggle that continues to this day.

And the women continued to make dough—the
kind of dough that rises to become a body-and soul-
warming staff of life, and the gold kind of dough
that builds and sustains a woman's right to live her
own life.

CHAPTER TEN

Manuella:
I Am a Fine-Looking Woman

**I am a fine-looking woman;
still I am running with my tears.**
—traditional song (Maidu)[1]

KP 98

The Grandmother watches intently the pattern of swirls of sand and water in her pan. As she swirls the sand and water, she lets the coarse grains on top escape. More water. More swirls. Finally, the heaviest particles remain. She searches for a glint of the metal she can trade for food at the white man's store in town.

No gold this time.

Again she swirls water and sand. Water and sand. Spirals of water and sand. As the sand circles around, her thoughts spiral back to a time when she and the other mothers and grandmothers lived on the land they knew so well. She thinks back to the time when her thoughts mattered. The time when she ran free. The time when the people she loved surrounded her. The time before her people's tears.

Those who came into her people's land called her Manuella. Her story gets confused with those of other Old Indian Women, most of whom were called "Old . . ." like Old Betsy and Old Limpy. Most of the old women were reported to be "over 100 years old."

Some said Manuella was born under the morning star in the month of waving grasses. They said that in the season when the oak leaves grew to the size of a rabbit's foot, Manuella would place a small sea shell in a basket. When she died, there were ninety-seven shells in her basket. But some said she was older even than that.

Manuella was so strong that she lived through the Gold Rush to old age. She lived on the outskirts of town near Mokelumne Hill in the southern Mother Lode country. One woman remembered that Manuella, unlike other Old Indian Women, "never wove baskets. The gold pan took its place."[2] Some believed she had magical powers to find gold.

Manuella's panning companion was a small black dog. The two would roam the hills, Manuella with a gold pan tucked under her arm, a tall walking stick in her hand. She wore a man's black hat tied under her chin with a string. And a man's coat, tied at the waist with a rope, over a long ruffled black calico dress.

Some recalled the time Manuella found the big one—a lump of gold big as a cocoanut, some marveled. She took her prize to a Mokelumne Hill gold buyer and opened an account. The deal was, he would keep the gold, and she would take out forty dollars when she needed it until its value was paid.

Both kept their part of the deal: the dealer kept her gold, and Manuella took the money out, forty dollars at a time, for several years. One day Manuella came in, took out her forty dollars and

Manuella

*Courtesy
Calaveras
County
Archives,
San Andreas, CA*

said, "That's all." The keeper of her gold checked his records, and they both agreed that Manuella had indeed drawn out the full value of her gold.

Some said Manuella was the daughter of a chief. Some insisted she was married to a chief, others to a medicine man. She must have been a powerful woman because some said she was a prophetess and that she presided over ceremonies. Manuella, the Prophetess. Queen Manuella. Manuella, Queen of her Tribe. Manuella, Queen of the Digger Indians.

The people who took over the Mother Lode country called the people who were there first "Digger Indians." They said the word with disgust

or with pity. Calling them Diggers made them something other than human, something to be pitied, if
not done away with.

There was no such tribe. The White Faces called
them Diggers because they dug in the earth for their
food. The women dug in the earth with sticks so the
land would live and provide the plants and grass
and ground cover that was right for that place.

> **The Indians never hurt anything, but
> the white people destroy all. They
> blast rocks and scatter them on the
> earth. The rocks say, 'Don't. You are
> hurting me.' But the white people pay
> no attention. . . . They don't care how
> much the ground cries out.**
> —from "The Ground Cries Out" (Wintu)[3]

The people who came into the country of
Manuella's people came only for the gold. They
lived freely on land that was not free.

What did they know of who Manuella was? What
do I know? Only what I have told. I can only imagine the rest.

I see in Manuella's face a quiet dignity, the
creases etched there by joy and pain. Much pain.
And memories terrible and serene.

*The Grandmother swirls water and sand. Water
and sand. Spirals of water and sand.*

Manuella learned meanings of ugly Anglo words
like malaria, small pox, venereal disease, massacre,
rape, kidnap, slave, lynch, bounty, treaty. Words
like extermination. And disposal. And inevitable.

One could say the "disposal" was mostly pas-
sive. Most Indian people of the Mother Lode died of

the diseases brought first by trappers and soldiers, then by the gold seekers. And for the rest, the meaning of words of men such as Senator J. J. Warner in 1852 was clear: "Better, far better, drive them at once into the ocean, or bury them in the land of their birth."[4]

Not only did the White Faces steal the Sierra people's water, they turned out their livestock on the land. The cattle ate plants used by the Indians and their game animals, leaving them nothing to eat. So when the Indians killed the cattle that came into the land the deer and rabbits once roamed, the miners treated them as thieves.

In 1848, Sierra Indians were more than half the gold miners, many of them women. Most Indians exchanged their gold for food and clothing and blankets. Some were virtual slaves. When the Oregonians arrived, they saw that whites exploiting Indian labor had an unfair advantage. And so the Oregonians began to chase the Indian people out. Retaliations built up. Treaties were useless because the Indian lands held gold.

The facts speak for what happened. Between 1845 and 1870, California's Indian population plummeted from an estimated one hundred and fifty thousand to less than thirty thousand.[5]

> **All cry! All cry!**
> **Last time for you to be sad.**
> —from "Summons to a Mourning Ceremony"
> by Chief Yanapayak (Miwok)[6]

So many people died that sounds of mourning ceremonies must have been heard above the din of picks and shovels and miners' voices. Survivors buried or cremated their dead and danced and sang and mourned for them.

Manuella's people kept and protected the wisdom of the ancestors acquired through thousands of years. It was a wisdom that kept them alert and alive to their world, intimately known to them.

The Grandmother swirls water and sand. Water and sand. Spirals of water and sand.

Manuella remembers living on the land with her people, hearing only the sounds of the earth and its creatures, the sounds of the voices of her people singing prayers and laughing, of rock on rock as the women pound and grind the acorns. She remembers the sounds of the evening as the ancient stories told by the grandmothers fade into the night cry of the coyote and the owl and the cricket.

From her grandmothers before her, she learned to watch the clouds and the sun and the shadows and the colors of the earth. She knew when her world would come alive and when it would die. She learned to know the season of flowering, the season of dry earth, the season of Big Times and of burning, and the season of snow. She learned where to find the plants, when to harvest the fruits of the earth, when to give thanks, and when to store.

The mothers and grandmothers made baskets essential to their people's survival. They made baskets for beating, gathering, and winnowing seeds, for ball game racquets, for trapping small game and fish, and for wearing as hats. Cool water washed their babies in small baskets suspended upright in clear creek pools. Large baskets called burden baskets, suspended from headbands around their foreheads held harvested crops and other items. Huge storage baskets could hold up to half a ton of food.

It was important for a woman to "keep her baskets right," for they determined a woman's worth. When she died, her baskets were destroyed.

I see the child Manuella before the coming of the White Faces. I see her running free, swimming in the water that ran clear, playing games with her friends, swinging on the yielding branches of the oak tree. I see her climbing the hills with the mothers and grandmothers to the special place where they will dig roots to dry for winter.

> **When I was a small girl, I went on root digging trips with my mother and helped her to collect plenty of roots to dry for winter use. These would be gathered in baskets. Some were cooked whole, or sometimes we pounded them up and cooked them like mush. . . .**
>
> —Marie Potts (Maidu)[7]

In the foothills of the Sierra Nevada lies a little valley that guards an oak-speckled meadow. In this meadow is Indian Grinding Rock (Chaw'se) State Historic Park. In the park is a re-created Miwok village, with slab houses, a ceremonial roundhouse, a game field, trails, a museum, and a camp ground.

The centerpiece of the park is the *chaw'se*—the grinding rock. In the massive limestone rock are hundreds of cuplike holes formed by the women pounding and grinding the acorns with elongated stones.

In the fall and early winter, Manuella's mothers and grandmothers gathered the acorns from the oak trees that covered the meadows and the low hills. Children and sometimes men helped with the harvest. They collected the harvest in burden bags woven by the mothers and the grandmothers, and spread their harvest in the sun to dry. What they didn't need immediately they stored indoors in huge baskets, or outdoors in bug-proof and water-

**Chaw'se, Indian Grinding Rock State Historic Park,
Pine Grove, CA**

proof granaries they called *cha'ka*. The mothers and grandmothers stored vast amounts of acorns to eat during winter, while the earth slept. The acorn was their gold.

The women shelled the acorns only as needed, then sat on the *chaw'se* and used their hand stones to crush and grind the acorns to meal *(pinole)* in the mortar cups. The rhythmic sounds of stone on stone merged with the women's prayer-songs to the sacred acorn.

Acorn meal is now known as some of the most nutritious food there is, but the tannin in raw acorn meal makes it bitter. So the women would leach out the bitterness by pouring hot, then cold water through the meal in a basin in sand lined with fern.

All come to the roundhouse for the First Fruits Ceremony! Give thanks to the earth for her gifts.

And so, Manuella's people feasted and danced and sang prayers to the spirits of the oak and its seeds, providers of yet another season of harvest.

Y-EHT-IM
TEH-LEI-LI!
Let us prepare
the new harvest
of acorn.[8]

From the acorn meal, the women made bread or cakes, and dried them in the sun. Or they baked the bread on a hot stone, or in hot ashes in an earth oven. They also made the acorn meal into soup or mush.

ACORN SOUP

Heat rocks in a fire and drop them
into a basket of acorn meal mixed
with water and perhaps pulp of
clover or dried, crushed wild berries.
Stir constantly until the hot rocks
heat the soup to a boil. Add more hot
rocks if necessary.

Each village had its own territory, which included several ecological zones of varied foods and animals. The people moved with the seasons, gathering the riches yielded by the earth to create and sustain life. They were not "migratory," wandering aimlessly around, as some described them. They simply had summer homes and winter homes.

The land was rich in offerings. Wild greens were steamed by pouring water around the edges of fire pits, or cooked with hot rocks in baskets. Roots and bulbs of sego and mariposa lilies, turnip and sweet potato were baked and eaten whole, or crushed and dried to make bread and cakes and medicines.

The mothers and grandmothers used elderberry and berries of the juniper and manzanita to make cider, jelly, wines, and medicines. They knew how to ferment it to make wines. Pounded and dried, the berries made good, portable cakes for traveling, or fruit soup in winter. Dried berries inside rattles entertained babies, sounded rhythm for dancing, or made fine decorations and jewelry.

The mothers and grandmothers know the ways that plants can heal. The aroma of crushed laurel leaves can cure a cold. Bark of the coffeeberry shrub works as a laxative or tonic, and sweet clover eaten raw cleanses the blood. The milky white sap of the milkweed can cleanse wounds, treat warts and ringworm. And it makes a good chewing gum. Bark of the choke cherry strengthens the voices of singers and speakers.

The mothers and grandmothers knew also the many uses of the soaproot. They could eat its leaves fresh, or bake and eat its roots. The leaves could be dried and used as a brush. The mashed root could be used as a poultice, as a cleanser, or to catch fish. Mixed with water, the crushed root releases the chemical saponin, which kills or stupefies the fish, which float to the surface, to be scooped up by hand and plopped into a basket.[9]

The men knew where the rabbits and deer and birds and fish lived, how to wait patiently to coax them to relinquish their lives. They knew how to protect their clan from outsiders. They knew how to burn the grass and the trees so new earth would grow. And they knew how to make prayers to the spirits in song and in dance, in their thoughts and their actions, so the spirits of the earth would continue to reveal and offer her gifts.

White men have fantasized about Indian women's subservience to men.

> For the Indian women are the
> patient, laboring and willing slaves of
> their lords—far more so than can be
> found in any portion of the white
> race on the race of the globe . . ..
> They do all the domestic drudgery,
> cook, cultivate . . ., do all the
> household labor, and, indeed carry
> all the burthens [sic]. The male, on
> the contrary, is 'monarch of all he
> surveys.'[10]

True, Indian women worked harder and longer than men—as they do around the world to this day. But women in most American Indian tribes had much more power within their communities than white men's laws and customs ever allowed women. Indian women carried more burdens, yes, but they usually owned and controlled those burdens—their houses and tools and the fruits of their own harvest. Further, as Sarah Winnemucca wrote of her Paiute sisters,

> The women know as much as the men
> do, and their advice is often asked.
> We have a republic as well as you.
> The Council-tent is our congress, and
> anybody can speak who has anything
> to say, women and all.[11]

The work is done! Gather at the game field for a ball game!

But it wasn't always just for fun. Sometimes it was played to determine status, or take the place of a fight or a war. Women played too, often with two or more balls—"wisdom-gathering," some called it.

The game was similar to soccer. Women could carry the ball but men could only kick it. But, a man could make a goal by picking up a woman holding a ball and carrying her across the line.

Manuella probably lived in a cone-shaped house *(u'macha')* of cedar poles covered with cedar slabs interwoven with willow or grape vines. The dwelling was much more than shelter. It was sacred space, for telling stories, eating sacred foods, and for ritual.

> **I . . . remember as a child living in the cedar bark house with my grandparents. How wonderful it was lying awake at night sometimes, to hear the coyotes bark, and the hoot owls uttering their calls among the trees. Sometimes there would be the running clatter of squirrels on the bark slabs above us; and in spring and summer, just as it grew light before the sun rose, there came the enchantment of the bird chorus, the orchestra of the Great Spirit all around us. That clean pine smell on the morning wind—where can we find it now?**
>
> —Marie Potts (Maidu)[12]

**Chaw'se,
Indian
Grinding
Rock State
Historic
Park, Pine
Grove, CA**

The spring of a young girl's life was a time of celebration and solemnity. A girl coming into womanhood would retreat to solitude and fasting. From the mothers and grandmothers, she would learn secrets of marriage and childbirth, and how to prevent conception.

The girl would perform rituals and tasks to prove that she was strong enough for a woman's roles. Once she had proven herself, the young woman's family would distribute gifts of food and the village would honor her with feasting and dancing.

Thou are a girl no more,
Thou are a girl no more; . . .
    Dance, dance,
    Dance, dance.
       —from "Puberty Dance Song" (Wintu)[13]

During their menses, women were not regarded as "unclean," as frequently reported by foreign observers. Rather, this was their most spiritually powerful time until they were old, when they were powerful all the time. Women had to be careful to use their power wisely.

For important events, the whole community would gather in the roundhouse. Before the coming of the White Faces, those who were able entered through a hole in the roof and descended a ladder into the womb-shaped roundhouse. It connected sky with earth, for it was in the roundhouse that male met female, birth met death, spirit met flesh.

The earth is round, and suspended by five ropes, say the Maidu ancestors. When the earth shakes, it is because an angry spirit is shaking the ropes.[14]

The female initiates and sustains, the male builds and protects. It is all part of a seamless essence where all is living, all is sacred. All in this world is alive. All has a soul. All is to be respected.

My words are tied in one
With the great mountains,
With the great rocks,
With the great trees,
In one with my body
And my heart.
       —from "Prayer for Good Fortune" (Yokuts)[15]

Moon, sun, earth, sky, stars and sea—all work together to sustain birth, life and death. There are those with special knowledge and skills who live and think between the worlds of spirit and earth, between earth and sky. They are the shamans, and some are women. Perhaps Manuella was a shaman, though most Miwok shamans were men. A shaman uses her great power, sometimes through dreams and hallucinations, to coax out bad spirits, like pain, and contact good spirits of the animals and the ancestors to know the right path.

When death came into their lands, Manuella and the other mothers keened and wailed to mourn the many who followed the spirit trail. But they knew that the spirits of their loved ones always were near.

Look up—there they are, in the Milky Way, the trail to the land of the dead. When someone dies, that person's soul continues on its path—the flower trail, the spirit trail.

Manuella, the Grandmother, knows that just as the moon dies and returns again to life, as the sun leaves the sky always to return, and as spring awakens the land, so does the human spirit abide.

Water and sand.
Spirals of water and sand.

POSTLUDE

Say Yes to One Another!

**At this eating assembled
you say 'yes' to one another!
Say 'yes' to one another!
Say 'yes' to one another!**
                —from "Feast Oration" (Wintu)[1]

After a gaunt winter, the sun now warms and ripens the earth. Spring colored grass carpets the ground, and tiny golden specks wink in the water. Birds and animals and miners who had fled the snows and winds of winter now return.

All winter, sheltered in their rock heated houses and eating only stored foods, the Sierra people have awaited the time when new clover covers the earth. The miners have kept going on the hope of things opening up in the spring.

Now, the earth awakens, and time and place mystically merge in a celebration of spring and renewal of hopes and dreams.

It is the month of May, Maya, or Mais—the Maiden of Spring. It is a season celebrated around the world since ancient times with feasting and dancing and making merry.

There's a festival in the meadow, and we're invited! We'll see a lot of people we know, so come along and join the fun.

Luzena Wilson, with help from her husband and several miners, is supervising the building of the long tables for this evening's feast. A Mother Lode band begins to tune up. There are fiddles and drums, trumpets and flutes, an Irish penny whistle, an accordion, and even a mandolin.

The center of the festivities is the May pole— ancient symbol of male sexuality, planted deep in Mother Earth. Indian people to the north dress their sacred pole in feathers. Our May pole is dressed in both feathers and ribbons. Dancing merrily around it are children dressed in new May clothes. The girls wear flowers in their hair.

Manuella is teaching dance steps to the children. The girl called Tom practices the steps, showing off the beautiful moccasins her father saved for her from the trail crossing. Martha Ross dances by, twirling in her new Chinese shawl. Lotta Crabtree giggles and sings as she invites Benjamin Bonney to dance with her. Warren Saddler and little Emma Griffis arrive, still searching for Emma's parents. Emma joins the dancing while Warren gets in on a kick ball game.

Doña Martinez rides by with her entourage. She grandly dismounts, and soon begins a slow, sensuous dance that becomes a fast fandango, red scarf whirling. More miners, hearing the merry sounds, have dropped their picks and shovels and are prancing around the May pole.

Simmering in the community pot is a multicultural stew—a potpourri of food from around the world to share when the evening's coolness descends.

Manuella has started the stew with acorn soup, to which she has added some wild onions. One of the miners throws in a liberal dose of whiskey.

We'll each contribute something from our heritage. I'll add German sausage and a touch of Cornish saffron. By the time we all give to the pot, we'll have a sumptuous blend of foods and cultures: Italian pasta, Greek olives, Mexican peppers, Hawaiian sweet potato, Chinese chestnuts, and generic miners' fare of potatoes, bacon, and beans.

The stew simmers while we join in on the dancing, read old letters, sing tunes from home, and catch up on news from friends old and new.

Here comes Marie Pantalon, dressed in her trademark pants and boots and ragged hat. She and André Douet have brought several cases of claret wine made from grapes grown in their vineyard. Following Marie and André is Clementine Brainard. She has brought little May baskets filled with spring flowers and sweets for the children, and a good amount of non-alcoholic punch for the miners.

Warren Saddler has spotted some color that looks like it could yield some gold, but instead he digs up what looks like the plum duff buried by the miner who failed to mix it right. Dame Shirley sweeps in to the party, notebook in hand, along with her cook, who contributes some real plum pudding.

Eliza Farnham arrives on horseback riding sidesaddle, ladylike, and grandly deposits loaves of perfect bread she has baked herself. An Australian miner shows off some damper he has steamed in an earth oven. He swears it tastes better than Eliza Farnham's bread.

Manuella has made some cakes of acorn flour,

water, and crushed berries. She and her sisters have smoked some fish over a smoldering fire.

The Monroe family arrives, dressed up for the occasion, bringing pies filled with walnuts from their sizeable orchard.

Lola Montez joins the dance around the May pole, coaching the giggling Lotta on her pirouettes. Lola has brought some of her famous German tea cakes, along with what she claims to be her receipt. No one knows for sure.

LOLA'S FAMOUS GOLD RUSH STYLE GERMAN TEA CAKES
(as the author imagines them to have been)

Combine 3 beaten eggs, 1 pound brown sugar, 1 teaspoon soda, and 1 teaspoon each cinnamon and cloves imported from the Far East. Let stand for an hour. Add a cup of raisins, which have been soaking in a cup of wine, and a cup of nuts. Mix well. Add 4 cups flour and 1 teaspoon baking powder and mix again. Pour the mixture into a large baking pan and bake for 30 minutes at a moderate temperature. While still warm, cut into bars and dredge in sugar if desired. These cakes will last for a long time if stored in a crock.

A cook from the Cary Hotel in Hangtown is whipping up some Hangtown Fry. Some miners have swiped some of the oysters to make oyster cocktail (oysters soaked in whiskey and spread with catsup, Worcestershire sauce, and pepper).

Juanita appears and joins the hurdy-gurdy girls

in a fetching dance. Juanita has brought *capirotada* (bread pudding) for the feast, and the hurdies contribute some sauerkraut.

Eliza Gregson has arrived from Sutter's Fort, with pasties (meat pie) from her mother's receipt. Her friends are showing off their latest quilt, while Captain Sutter spins tales of the good old days for the children, and James Marshall sells his autograph.

All is ready for the feast. But before the eating begins, the chief invokes the blessing:

> **At this eating assembled**
> **you say 'yes' to one another!**

And so, in this magical month, at this fantastic place, where time and place mystically mingle, these people have gathered. Some have been here for a long time, while others have journeyed from far away to come to this golden land. All have lived to embrace once more the promise of spring—a spring colored green and gold.

Evening begins to descend on Mother Lode. Frogs and crickets strike up a chorus of night sounds. A coyote lifts a lonely howl to the sky.

And the voices sound together.

> **Say 'yes' to one another!**
> **Say 'yes' to one another!**

ENDNOTES

INTRODUCTION:
1. Beasley, p. 18.
2. Beasley, p. 18.
3. Marks, p. 170.
4. Eargle, p. 20.
5. Margolin, p. 6.
6. Colonel Richard B. Mason, military governor of California, cited in Dillinger, p. 13.
7. Marks, p. 250.

MANUELLA'S SONG:
1. Merriam.

CHAPTER ONE:
1. Quoted in C. Hart Merriam, *The Dawn of the World: Tales of the Miwok Indians of California, 1910.*
2. Lothrop, p. 14.
3. Merriam-Webster, p. 179.
4. Hulbert, p. 5.
5. Jeffrey, p. 8.

CHAPTER TWO:
1. Bonney, p. 39.
2. Heinrich Leinhard, Sutter's Fort State Historic Park.
3. Quoted in Garoutte, p. 57.
4. Curran, p. 72.
5. Quoted in Dillinger, p. 11.
6. Paul, p. 176.
7. *The Land of Gold: Three Years in California, 1850* as quoted in Quaife, p. 158.
8. Quaife, p. xv.
9. Quaife xvi.
10. Time-Life Books, 1974, p. 32.

CHAPTER THREE:
1. Time-Life Books, 1978, p. 43.
2. Quaife, p. 160.
3. Ogden, p. 13.
4. "Duff" is a supposedly edible bread-like food, probably named after decaying organic matter on a forest floor. See Chapter 5.

5. Quoted in Hulbert, p. 183.

CHAPTER FOUR:
1. The line drawings in this chapter are by Kathryn Uhl, from *Luzena Stanley Wilson '49er,* 1937.

CHAPTER FIVE:
1. Bates, p. 221.
2. Duffy, p. 10.
3. Duffy, p. 10.
4. Crosley-Griffin, p. 8.
5. Haskins, p. 294.
6. Erdoes, p. 42.
7. "Receipt" adapted from California Heritage Cook Book, Junior League, distributed by El Dorado County Historical Society.
8. Gentry, p. 38.
9. Comstock, 1982, p. 383.
10. Robinson, p. 461.
11. Mather, p. 21.
12. Quoted in Jackson, p. 171.
13. Wedlake.
14. Phillips, 119.
15. Foley.
16. Sheafer, p. 69.
17. Constance Rourke, *Troupers of the Gold Coast: or The Rise of Lotta Crabtree,* quoted in Jackson, p. 197.

CHAPTER SIX:
1. De Ferrari, p. 588.
2. Perlo, p. xx.
3. Mather, p. 17.
4. Rohrbough, p. 154.
5. Adapted from *Ethnic Heritage Cookbook,* p. 27.

CHAPTER SEVEN:
1. Chandler, p. 6.
2. Quoted in Anderson, Vol. 1, p. 477.
3. Anderson II, 147.
4. George Sand, *My Life,* quoted in Anderson, Vol. 2, p. 147.

5. Greer, p. 58.
6. Phillips, p. 160.
7. Curtis, p. 4.
8. Jackson, p. 165.
9. Guerin, p. 22.
10. Phillips, p. 162.
11. Jensen and Lothrop, p. 9.
12. Herman, p. 28.
13. Herman, p. 29.

CHAPTER EIGHT:
1. Werner, p. 1.
2. Luchetti, p. 71.

CHAPTER NINE:
1. Haskins, p. 73.
2. Perlot, p. 246.
3. Phillips, p. 116.
4. Ripley, p. 34.
5. Quoted in Hays, ed., p. 214.
6. Rohrbough, p. 184.
7. Brown, p. 16.
8. Jensen, p. 16.
9. French, p. 188.

CHAPTER TEN:
1. Amanda Wilson, quoted in Margolin, p. 29.
2. McMillian.
3. Kate Luckie, quoted in Margolin, p. 179.
4. Quoted in Comstock, 1987, p. 56.
5. Rawls, p. 171.
6. Quoted in Margolin, p. 85.
7. Quoted in Margolin, p. 16.
8. *The Indian Historian.*
9. Chaw'se.
10. "Scenes in California."
11. Sarah Winnemucca Hopkins, *Life Among the Piutes [sic]: Their Wrongs and Claims,* 1883.
12. Quoted in Margolin, p. 16.
13. Quoted in Margolin, p. 22.
14. Baggelmann.
15. Quoted in Margolin, p. 98.

POSTLUDE:
1. Quoted in Margolin, p. 61.

ACKNOWLEDGMENTS

The following have provided valuable information and assistance:

Lanette Smith
Ed Tyson, Searls Historical Library
Katie Hagen, Tigard Library, Tigard, Oregon
Virginia McElroy and Caroline Lieberman, California
    Heritage Quilt Project
Ande Schweiker, Mariposa Museum and History Center
Multnomah County Library, Portland
Flora Jane Gorman
Sheryl Waller, Calaveras County Historical Society, San
    Andreas
Sherrin Grout, Columbia State Historic Park
Chaw'se Regional Indian Museum, Pine Grove
Tuolumme County Museum and History Center, Sonora
California State Library, Sacramento
State of California Department of Parks and Recreation

The author wishes to thank Larry Cenotto, Archivist for the Amador County Museum and Archives, for introducing me to Marie Pantalon, and for sharing with me his considerable research on her story.

Thanks also to Monique Fillion of Thônes, France, for her research and valuable feedback.

CREDITS

Permission has been granted to publish photographs from the following:

California Heritage Quilt Project
Calaveras County Archives, San Andreas
Calaveras County Historical Society, San Andreas
Les Amis du Val de Thônes, Thônes, France
El Dorado County Museum, Placerville
Searls Historical Library, Nevada City
Flora Jane Gorman
Tuolumne County Museum and History Center, Sonora
Coulterville Chronicle, Northern Mariposa County
   History Center, Coulterville
Marshall Gold Discovery State Historic Park, Coloma
State of California Department of Parks & Recreation
California State Library, Sacramento

Permission has been granted to quote material from the following:

Eliza Gregson. "The Gregson Memoirs Containing Mrs. Eliza Gregson's 'Memory' and the Statement of James Gregson." Reprinted from *California Historical Society Quarterly,* XIX, No. 2 (June 1940).

Margaret Frink. *Covered Wagon Women: Diaries and Letters from the Western Trails, 1840–1890.* Kenneth L. Holmes, ed. Spokane, WA: Arthur H. Clark, 1983–1993.

Warren Sadler. *Warren Sadler Journal, reminiscences, and miscellaneous paper, 1849–1867* (BANC MSS C–F 73), The Bancroft Library, University of California, Berkeley.

Clementine A. Brainard. *Journal, 1853–1855.* Ellen August Sears. "Interesting Excerpts from Auto-biography of Ellen August Sears." California State Parks, Columbia State Historic Park, Columbia.

Excerpts. *The Way We Lived: California Indian Stories, Songs & Reminiscences.* California Historical Society, 1981, 1993.

Mary Ballou and Abby Mansur. *Let Them Speak for Themselves: Women in the American West, 1849–1900,* edited by Christiane Fischer ©1977 by The Shoe String Press, Inc. Reprinted by permission of Archon Books/The Shoe String Press, Inc., North Haven, Connecticut.

BIBLIOGRAPHY

"Acorn Food was Basic Necessity . . ." *The Indian Historian,* I, No. 1 (October 1964).

Allen, Judy. "Children on the Overland Trails." *Overland Journal,* 12, No. 1 (Spring 1994), 2–11.

Anderson, Bonnie S. and Judith P. Zinsser. *A History of Their Own: Women in Europe,* Vol. I and II. NY: Harper & Row, 1988.

Baggelmann, Ted. "Adobe, Gold and Stone." *California Indians. The Daily Union Democrat,* Sonora (Tuolumne County) CA, December 26, 1947.

Ballou, Mary. "I Hear the Hogs in My Kitchen." Fischer, 1977, 42–47.

Bancroft, Hubert H. *History of the Pacific States of North America,* Vol. VI, 1848–1859. San Francisco: The History Company, 1888.

Bates, Mrs. D.B. *Incidents on Land and Water, or Four Years on the Pacific Coast.* Boston: James French and Company, 1858.

Berkla, Dennis. "Were Hernan de Soto's Men the First Spaniards in California?" The Californians, 9, No. 4 (Jan./Feb. 1992), 8–16.

Beasley, Delilah. *The Negro Trail Blazers of California.* NY: Negro Universities Press, 1919, 1969.

Black, Eleanora and Sidney Robertson. *The Gold Rush Song Book.* San Francisco: The Colt Press, 1940.

Blevins, Winfred. *Dictionary of the American West.* NY: Facts On File, 1993.

Bowes, Kathleen. "The Woman Suffrage Movement in Nevada County, California: 1869–1911." *Nevada County Historical Society Bulletin,* 46, No. 2 (April 1992), 9–14.

Brainard, Clementine A. *Journal, 1853–1855.* Reproduced from an original in the archives, Department of Parks and Recreation, Columbia State Historic Park.

Brown, Cleo Elaine. "Foregotten [sic] Survivalists." Unpublished paper. Calaveras County Historical Society, 1986–87.

Browne, Juanita Kennedy. *Nuggets of Nevada County History.* Nevada City, CA: Nevada County Historical Society, 1983.

Bruff, J. Goldsborough. *Gold Rush: The Journals, Drawings, and other Papers of J. Goldsborough Bruff.* Read, Georgia Willis and Ruth Gaines, eds. NY: Columbia University Press, 1949.

Burrows, Jack. "Digger! The Vanished Miwoks of California." *Montana The Magazine of Western History,* XXI, No. 1 (Winter 1971), 28–39.

Butruille, Susan G. *Women's Voices from the Oregon Trail.* Boise, ID: Tamarack Books, Inc., 1993; 2nd Edition, 1994.

————. *Women's Voices from the Western Frontier.* Boise, ID: Tamarack Books, Inc., 1995.

Calhoon, F.D. *Coolies, Kanakas and Cousin Jacks.* Sacramento, CA: F.D. Calhoon, 1986. 2nd Ed. 1995.

Carpenter, Helen. *A Trip Across the Plains in an Ox Cart, 1857. Women's Overland Diaries from the Huntington Library.* Sandra L. Myres, ed. San Marino: Huntington Library, 1980.

Castillo, Edward. "The Other Side of the 'Christian Curtain': California Indians and the Missionaries." *The Californians,* 10, No. 2 (Sept./Oct. 1992), 9–17.

Cenotto, Larry. Jackson, CA. Interviews: June 1997, March 1998.

"Chaw'se Indian Grinding Rock State Historic Park." Pamphlet. California State Department of Parks & Recreation, 1994.

Chandler, Dr. Robert J. "Emma Hardinge: A Spiritual Voice for the Slave and the Union." *Dogtown Territorial Quarterly,* No. 29 (Spring 1997), 31+.

Chidsey, Donald Barr. *The California Gold Rush.* NY: Crown Publishers, 1968.

Clappe, Louise (Dame Shirley). *The Shirley Letters.* Salt Lake City: Peregrine Smith Books, 1983. First published serially in *The Pioneer Magazine,* 1854–55.

Comstock, David Allan. *Brides of the Gold Rush: The Nevada County Chronicles 1851–1859.* Grass Valley: Comstock Bonanza Press, 1987.

————. *Gold Diggers and Camp Followers: The Nevada County Chronicles 1845–51.* Grass Valley: Comstock Bonanza Press, 1982 and 1988.

Cooke, Lucy Rutledge. *Crossing the Plains in 1852: Narrative of a Trip from Iowa to "The Land of Gold," as Told in Letters Written During the Journey.* Fairfield, WA: Ye Galleon Press, 1987.

————. *Letters on the Way to California. Covered Wagon Women: Diaries & Letters from the Western Trails, 1852.* Vol. IV, *The California Trail.* Kenneth L. Holmes, Ed. Bison Books Edition. Lincoln and London: University of Nebraska Press, 1997.

Costello, Julia. "Apautawilu: A Miwok Village in Calaveras County." VF Indians, Calaveras County Museum, n.d.

Crosley-Griffin, Mary. *Hangtown (Tales of Old Placerville).* Universal City, CA: Crosley Books, 1994.

Cummings, Mariett Foster. *A Trip Across the Continent. Covered Wagon Women: Diaries & Letters from the Western Trails, 1852.* Vol. IV, *The California Trail.* Kenneth L. Holmes, Ed. Bison Books Edition. Lincoln and London: University of Nebraska Press, 1997.

Curran, Harold. *Fearful Crossing: The Central Overland Trail Through Nevada.* Las Vegas: Nevada Publications, 1982.

Curtis, Mabel Rowe. *The Coachman Was A Lady.* Watsonville, CA: Pajaro Valley Historical Association, 1959.

Davis, Sara. Diary. *Nevada County Historical Society Bulletin,* 45, No. 2–3 (April, July 1991), 17–19.

De Ferrari, Carlo M., Sonora, CA. Telephone interview, March 1998.

————. "The Ethnic Argonauts." *CHISPA, The Quarterly of the*

Tuolumne County Historical Society, Sonora, CA, 17, No. 3 (January-March 1978), 585–591.

DeGraaf, Lawrence B. "Race, Sex, and Region: Black Women in the American West, 1850–1920." *Pacific Historical Review,* 49, No. 2 (May 1980), 285–313.

"Description of Towns in 1850: Nevada City." *Nevada County Historical Society Bulletin,* 45, No. 2–3 (April, July 1991), 19–20.

"Des Millions Pour un Sou! Mines D'Or de la Californie," French Poster on the Gold Rush, 1849. Translation Lanette Smith. Phillips, 1942, 1978.

Dexter, John L. "Mariposa On The Mother Lode." *Mariposa Gazette 1854–1979,* 34–35. First published in 1938.

Dillinger, William C. *The Gold Discovery: James Marshall and the California Gold Rush.* Santa Barbara, CA: Sequoia Communications, 1990.

Dutschke, Arlene. Ranger, Chaw'se, Indian Grinding Rock State Historic Park. Interview, June 1997.

Douglas, Belle. "The Last of the Oustomahs." *Nevada County Historical Society Bulletin,* 13, No. 4 (March 1960). Published 1921.

Duchow, John C. "Terrible Excitement in Columbia—Murder of J. H. Smith of Knickerbocker Flat." *Columbia Gazette,* 13 October, 1855. Reproduced from an original in the archives, Department of Parks and Recreation, Columbia State Historic Park.

Duffy, John. "Medicine in the West: An Historical Overview." *Journal of the West* (July 1982), 5–14.

"E.W." Letter from California. Stanislaus Diggings, Aug. 4, 1849. *CHISPA, the Quarterly of the Toulumne County Historical Society,* 20, No. 4 (April-June 1981), 693–696.

Eargle, Dolan H., Jr. *The Earth Is Our Mother: A Guide to the Indians of California, Their Locales and Historic Sites.* San Francisco: Trees Company Press, 1986.

"Emigrants De La Vallée De Thônes Dans Le Monde." *Amis du Val De Thônes.* Translation Lanette Smith. VF Marie Suize Pantalon.

Erdoes, Richard. *Saloons of the Old West.* NY: Alfred A. Knopf, 1979.

Ethnic Heritage Cookbook. Northern Mariposa County History Center. Coulterville, CA: Bald Mountain Press, 1992.

Evans, Robert Gage. "The Rocker." *The Californians,* II, No. 6, 37–40.

Fariss & Smith. Excerpt from *History of Plumas, Lassen & Sierra Counties,* 1882. Sierra County Museum.

Farnham, Eliza W. *California In-doors and Out (1856).* Facsimile. Introduction by Madeleine B. Stern. Pub. by B. DeGraaf Nieukoop, 1972.

Farquhar, Francis P., ed. *Luzena Stanley Wilson, '49er.* Mills College, CA: The Eucalyptus Press, 1937.

Fillion, Monique, Thônes, France. Letter, March 16, 1998.

Fischer, Christiane, ed. *Let Them Speak for Themselves: Women in the American West,* 1849–1900. Archon Books, 1977.

Fisher, Vardis and Opal Laurel Holmes. *Gold Rushes and Mining Camps of the Early American West.* Caldwell, ID: Caxton Printers, Ltd., 1968.

Fletcher, Jack E. and Patricia K.A. "The Cherokee Trail." *Overland Journal,* 13, No. 2 (1995), 21–33.

French, Marilyn. *Beyond Power.* NY: Summit Books, 1985.

"The French War." *Historical Bulletin,* Calaveras County Historical Society, San Andreas, CA,1, No. 3 (April 1953), 3.

Frink, Margaret A. *Adventures of a Party of Gold-seekers. Covered Wagon Women: Diaries & Letters from the Western Trails, 1840-1890.* Vol. II, 1850. Kenneth L. Holmes, Ed. Glendale, CA: The Arthur H. Clark Company, 1983.

"From the New Route—Ball at Relief Camp Sonora, Oct. 6th, 1853." *San Joaquin Republican,* October 11, 1853. VF, Tuolomne County Historical Society, Sonora.

Frye, L. Thomas, Director, California Gold Rush Sesquicentennial Project and Chief Curator Emeritus of History, Oakland Museum. Telephone Interview, February 1998.

Garoutte, Sally. "California's First Quilting Party." *Uncoverings 1981, Vol. 2 of the Research Papers of the American Quilt Study Group.* Sally Garoutte, ed. San Francisco: American Quilt Study Group, 1982.

Gentry, Curt. *The Madams of San Francisco: An Irreverent History of the City by the Golden Gate.* NY: Ballantine Books, 1964.

Gillet, Felix. Translated by Lauren Davis, Guy Albert and Christian Siedenburg. "The Indians of California." *Nevada County Historical Society Bulletin,* 42, No. 3 (July 1988), 20–23. Originally published in a French journal, 1874.

Glass, Paul and Louis C. Singer. *Songs of Town and City Folk.* NY: Grosset & Dunlap, 1967.

———. *Songs of Hill and Mountain Folk.* NY: Grosset & Dunlap, 1967.

Gold Rush Country: Guide to California's Mother Lode & Northern Mines. Sunset Books and Sunset Magazine, ed. Menlo Park, CA: Lane Publishing Co., 1957.

Gradon, Charles K. "The Emigrant Trail Through Nevada City, California." *Nevada County Historical Society Bulletin,* 45, No. 2–3 (April, July 1991), 10–17.

Greer, Germaine. *The Obstacle Race.* NY: Farrar Straus Giroux, 1979.

Gregson, Eliza and James. "The Gregson Memoirs Containing Mrs. Eliza Gregson's 'Memory' and the Statement of James Gregson." Reprinted from *California Historical Society Quarterly,* XIX, No. 2 (June, 1940).

Gudde, Erwin G. "The Name California." *Names: Journal of the American Name Society,* II, No. 2 (June 1954),121–133.

Guerin, Mrs. E.J. *Mountain Charley or the Adventures of Mrs. E.J. Guerin, Who was Thirteen Years in Male Attire.* University of Oklahoma Press, 1968.

Harrison, Wendy. "Bountiful Land: A Guide to the Miwok Plant Trail." Pamphlet. Chaw'se Association, 1991.

Haskins, C.W. *The Argonauts of California: Being the Reminiscences of Scenes and Incidents that Occurred in California in Early Mining Days.* NY: Fords, Howard & Hulbert, 1890.

Haun, Catherine. "A Woman's Trip Across the Plains in 1849." See Schlissel, 1982, 166–185.

Herman, Daniel. "Science, Seance and San Francisco: The Spiritualists' Phantom Fandango." *The Californians,* 11, No. 2, 18–37.

Hislop, Donald and Benjamin M. Hughes. "Gold Rush Gambling, Chapter 4, Games & Ladies & Cheating." *Dogtown Territorial Quarterly,* No. 29 (Spring 1997), 12–13+.

Holmes, Kenneth L., ed. *Covered Wagon Women: Diaries and Letters from the Western Trails, 1840–1890.* Spokane, WA: Arthur H. Clark, 1983–1993.

———. Vol. 4, *The California Trail.* Lincoln and London: University of Nebraska Press, 1997.

Hulbert, Archer Butler. *Forty-Niners: The Chronicle of the California Trail.* Boston: Little, Brown, and Company, 1931.

The Indian Historian. American Indian Historical Society, 1, No. 1 (October 1964).

Jackson, Joseph Henry. *Anybody's Gold: The Story of California's Mining Towns.* NY and London: D. Appleton-Century Company, Inc., 1941.

James, Mrs. Harry. "Indians of Mokelumne Hill." VF Indians, Calaveras County Museum, n.d.

Janicot, Michel. *The Ladies of the Night: A Short History of Prostitution in Nevada County, California.* Nevada City, CA: Mountain House Books, 1986, 1996.

Jeffrey, Julie Roy. *Frontier Women: The Trans-Mississippi West, 1840–1880.* NY: Hill and Wang, 1979.

Jensen, Joan M. and Gloria Ricci Lothrop. *California Women: A History.* San Francisco: Boyd & Fraser Publishing Company, 1987.

Jones, Pat. "The Forgotten Pioneer: Simmon Pena Storms." *Nevada County Historical Society Bulletin,* 37, No. 4 (October 1983), 26–31.

Katz, William Loren. *The Black West.* Anchor Books, 1973.

Kirkpatrick, Jean. "The Sheepranch Indians." VF Indians, Calaveras County Museum, n.d.

Krull, Kathleen. "Calafia, the Queen of California." *The Californians,* 11, No. 3, 21–23.

Laury, Jean Ray and the California Heritage Quilt Project. *Ho for California! Pioneer Women and Their Quilts.* NY: E.P. Dutton, 1990.

Lavender, David. *The Overland Migrations: Settlers to Oregon, California, and Utah.* Washington, DC: US Department of the Interior National Park Service, n.d.

Levy, Jo Ann. *They Saw the Elephant: Women in the California Gold Rush.* OK: University of Oklahoma Press, 1992.

Levy, Richard. "Eastern Miwok." VF Indians, Calaveras County Museum, n.d.

Linsenmeyer, Helen Walker. "From Fingers to Finger Bowls, Part I: The Pre-Mission Indians." From "California Cookery." *The Californians,* 9, No.4, 50–51.

———. "From Fingers to Finger Bowls: Part IV: The Bear-Eating Gold seekers." Excerpt from the book. *The Californians,* 10, No. 1 (July/August 1992), 48–50.

Lockley, Fred, ed. "Recollections of Benjamin Franklin Bonney."
    Oregon Historical Quarterly, 24 (March 1923), 36–55.
Loomis, Rev. A.W. "Chinese Women in California." *The Overland
    Monthly* (September 1869), 237–331.
Loomis, Rev. A.W. "Chinese Proverbs." *The Overland Monthly,* 10, No.
    1 (January 1873), 82–85.
Lothrop, Gloria Ricci. "Westering Women and the Ladies of Los Angeles:
    Sisters Under the Skin?" *The Californians,* 12, No. 6, 12–23.
Luchetti, Cathy. *Home on the Range: A Culinary History of the
    American West.* NY: Villard Books, 1993.
MacDonald, Craig. *Cockeyed Charley Parkhurst, The West's Most
    Unusual Stagewhip.* Palmer Lake, CO: Filter Pres, 1973.
"Madam Lola." Compiled by Doris Foley. *Nevada County Historical
    Society,* 6, No. 6 (December 1952).
"Madame Moustache," VF, Searls Historical Library, Nevada City.
Maino, Jeannette Gould. *Left Hand Turn: A Story of the Donner Party
    Women.* n.p. 1987.
Maniery, James Gary. "Kosoimuno-nu (Six-Mile Rancheria)." *Las
    Calaveras, Quarterly Bulletin of the Calaveras County Historical
    Society,* XXXII, No. 2 (January 1984), 11–20.
Maniery, James Gary and Dwight Dutschke. "Northern Miwok at Big
    Bar: A Glimpse into the Lives of Pedro and Lily O'Connor." *The
    Californians,* 10, No.1 (July/August 1992), 28–31.
Mansur, Abby. "Letters Written to Her Sister, 1852–1854." Fischer,
    1977, 48–57.
"Manuella Jesus." Panama Pacific Exposition of Calaveras County
    (1915), 5–6. VF Indians. Calaveras County Historical Society.
Margolin, Malcolm, ed. *The Way We Lived: California Indian Stories,
    Songs & Reminiscences.* Berkeley: Heyday Books, California
    Historical Society, 1981, 1993.
"Marie Pantalon, Mort de." *L'Industriel Savoisien,* 1892. Translation
    Jacqueline Brodnitz.
Marks, Paula Mitchell. *Precious Dust. The American Gold Rush Era:
    1848–1900.* NY: William Morrow and Company, Inc., 1994.
Mather, R.E. "Borthwick's California: Gold Rush Panorama." *The
    Californians: The Magazine of California History,* 12, No.1, 16–25.
Mattes, Merrill J. *The Great Platte River Road.* Nebraska State Historical
    Society, 1969.
McMillian, Cecille Vandell. "Queen Manuella." *Las Calaveras,
    Quarterly Bulletin of the Calaveras County Historical Society,* No.
    2 (January 1953).
Merriam, C. Hart. *The Dawn of the World: Tales of the Miwok Indians
    of California.* Originally published by Arthur H. Clark, 1910;
    reprinted by University of Nebraska, 1993.
Merriam-Webster. *Webster's Guide to American History.* Springfield,
    MA: G.& C. Merriam Company, 1971.
Miller, Joaquin. "Isles of the Amazons." *The Overland Monthly,* 9, No.
    3 (September 1872), 201–207, 278–282; 9, No. 4 (October 1872),
    297–304; 9, No. 5 (November 1872), 393–401; 9, No. 6 (December
    1872), 489–497;10, No. 1 (January 1873), 9–15.

Miller, Ronald Dean. *Shady Ladies of the West.* Los Angeles: Westernlore Press, 1964.

Monson, Albert. "The Mysterious Indian of Grass Valley." *San Francisco Chronicle,* August 3, 1896. Nevada County Historical Society, 5, No. 2 (March 1951).

Moore, John. 6th Grade San Andreas Elementary. "Limpy, Her Story." VF Indians, Calaveras County Museum, n.d.

"Mountaineer." "From the New Route—Ball at Relief Camp, Sonora, Oct. 6th, 1853." *San Joaquin Republican* (October 11, 1853). Reprinted Tuolumne County Historical Society, Sonora, CA.

Murphy, Virginia Reed. *Across the Plains in the Donner Party.* Silverthorne, CO: Vistabooks, 1995.

Myres, Sandra L., ed. *Ho for California: Women's Overland Diaries from the Huntington Library.* San Marino, CA: Huntington Library, 1980.

Neithammer, Carolyn. *American Indian Food and Lore.* NY: Collier Books/Macmillan Publishing Company, 1974.

Ogden, Annegret. "A Dream that almost came true: Afro-American Voices during the California Gold Rush, Part I—The Voice of Rachel Ann Brown." *The Californians,* 8, No. 5 (January-February 1991), 12–13.

Paul, Rodman W. *The California Gold Discovery.* Georgetown, CA: The Talisman Press, 1967.

Pennebaker, G.W. "Romance of Chutkaya, the Queen of her Tribe." *Calaveras Weekly* (February 13, 1943). VF Indians, Calaveras County Museum.

Perlot, Jean-Nicholas. *Gold Seeker: Adventures of a Belgian Argonaut during the Gold Rush Years.* Helen Harding Bretnor, translator. Howard R. Lamar, ed. New Haven and London: Yale University Press, 1985.

Perkins, Elisha Douglass. *Gold Rush Diary: Being the Journal of Elisha Douglass Perkins on the Overland Trail in the Spring and Summer of 1849.* Clark, Thomas D., ed. Lexington: University of Kentucky Press, 1967.

Phillips, Catherine Coffin. *Coulterville Chronicle: The Annals of a Mother Lode Mining Town.* San Francisco: The Grabhorn Press, 1942. Fresno: Valley Publishers, 1978.

Quaife, Milo Milton, ed. *Pictures of the California Gold Rush.* Chicago: The Lakeside Press, R.R. Donnelley & Sons Co. Christmas, 1949.

Rawls, James J. *Indians of California: The Changing Image.* OK: University of Oklahoma Press, 1984.

Riley, Glenda. "American Daughters: Black Women in the West." *Black Women in American History.* Darlene Clark Hine, ed. Brooklyn: Carlson Publishing, 1990.

Ripley, Homer. *Not a History of Columbia.* Columbia, CA: IBEX Designs, 1986.

———. "Pan Bread, Beans and Miner's Pie." Pamphlet. Homer Ripley, 1990.

Robinson, Henry. "Pioneer Days of California." *The Overland Monthly,* 8, No. 5 (May 1872), 457–462.

Rolfe, Emily Lindsey. "Reminscences of Emily Lindsey Rolfe." *Nevada County Historical Society Bulletin*, 20, No. 4 (December 1966).

Rorhbough, Malcolm J. *Days of Gold: The California Gold Rush and the American Nation.* Berkeley: University of California Press, 1997.

Ross, Jennie E. "A Child's Experience in '49 As Related by Mrs. M.A. Gentry of Oakland, Cal." *The Overland Monthly,* LXIII, No. 3, 300–305; No. 4, 402–408; No. 5, 505–511.

Saddler, Warren. "Reminiscences." Manuscript C-F, Vol. I. Bancroft Library, University of California Berkeley.

Savage, William Sherman. *Blacks in the West.* Westport, CN: Greenwood Press, 1976.

Schlissel, Lillian. *Women's Diaries of the Westward Journey.* NY: Schocken Books, 1982.

"Scenes in California." Gleason's Pictorial Drawing-Room Companion, n.d. 125th Commemmoration Issue—*Mariposa Gazette,* 1854–1979.

"Sears, Aldem (Alden)." Reproduced from an original in the archives, Department of Parks and Recreation, Columbia State Historic Park.

Sears, Ellen August. "Interesting Excerpts from Autobiography of Ellen August Sears." Reproduced from archives, Department of Parks and Recreation, Columbia State Historic Park.

Sheafer, Silvia Anne. *Women of the West.* Reading, MA: Addison-Wesley Publishing Company, Inc., 1980.

Simmons, Alexy. *Red Light Ladies: Settlement Patterns and Material Culture on the Mining Frontier.* Anthropology Northwest, No. 4. Corvallis, OR: Oregon State University Department of Anthropology, 1984.

Solano, Isidora. "Reminiscences of A Princess, Isidora Solano." Introduction by Gloria Ricci Lothrop. *The Californians,* 11, No. 3, 24–28.

Suize, Marie Pantalon. VF, Amador County Archives and Museum.

Sunset Books and Sunset Magazine, ed. *Gold Rush Country: Guide to California's Mother Lode & Northern Mines.* Menlo Park, CA: Lane Publishing Co., 1957.

Sutter's Fort State Historic Park, Sacramento, CA.

Time-Life Books. *The Forty-Niners.* NY: Time-Life Books, 1974.

———. *The Old West: The Gamblers.* Alexandria, VA, 1978.

———. *The Wild West.* Warner Books, n.d.

Tinloy, Patrick. "Nevada County's Chinese," Part 1. *Nevada County Historical Society Bulletin,* 25, No. 1 (January 1971), 1–3.

Trager, James. *The People's Chronology.* NY: Henry Holt and Company, Inc., 1992.

———. *The Women's Chronology.* NY: Henry Holt and Company, Inc., 1994.

Trafzer, Clifford E. *California Indians and the Gold Rush.* Newcastle, CA: Sierra Oaks Publishing Company, 1989.

"Truckee." *Nevada County Historical Society Bulletin,* 2, No. 5 (October 1949).

"The Up and Down Life of Sarah Wallis." *The Californians,* 11, No. 15 (1994), 22.

Waldner, Lucile Marshall. *Gold Rush Recipes With the Secret Ingredient.* Van Nuys, CA: Creative Book Company, 1978.

Wedlake, Ron. Grass Valley, California. Telephone interview, June 1997.

Walker, Barbara G. *The Woman's Encyclopedia of Myths and Secrets.* NY: Harper & Row, 1983.

Watson, Jeanne Hamilton, ed. *To the Land of Gold and Wickedness: The 1848–59 Diary of Lorena L. Hays.* St. Louis: The Patrice Press, 1988.

Werner, Emmy E. *Pioneer Children on the Journey West.* Boulder, San Francisco, Oxford: Westview Press, 1995.

Whipple-Haslam, Mrs. Lee. *Early Days in California: Scenes and Events of the '50s as I remember Them.* Jamestown, CA: The Mother Lode Magnet, 1925.

Wierzbicki, Felix Paul. Introduction by Alicja Pomian-Pozerska. "California As It Is And As It May Be," 1849. From "Tales of the Pioneers, Part II: The Gold Region." *The Californians,* 12, No. 3, 41–46.

Wilson, Eleanor D. "Schliemann Slept Here." *Dogtown Territorial Quarterly,* No. 14 (Summer 1993), 6–7+.

Willieme, Andre. "California: Stalking the Origins of a Singular Name." *The Californians,* 11, No. 3, 16–21.

Winnemucca, Sarah. Mrs. Horace Mann, ed. *Life Among the Piutes [sic]: Their Wrongs and Claims.* NY: Putnam's Sons, 1883.

Zanjani, Sally. *A Mine of Her Own: Women Prospectors in the American West, 1850–1950.* Lincoln, NE: University of Nebraska Press, 1997.

Zumwalt, Eve Starcevick. *The Romance of Mokelumne Hill: A Pageant of History.* Fresno: Pioneer Publishing Co., 1990.

INDEX

ABOUT THE AUTHOR

Susan Butruille has been mining nuggets of women's history for more than twenty years, producing three books in the *Women's Voices* series, numerous speeches, editorship of a needle arts magazine, and an award-winning column for *The Woman's Journal*. *Women's Voices from the Oregon Trail* was the first book published by Tamarack Books, Inc., in 1993. *Women's Voices from the Western Frontier* was a 1996 Oregon Book Awards finalist in Literary Nonfiction. Born in Colorado, Susan Butruille has lived in several states including Alaska, and now makes her home in the Portland area. Susan has created a one-woman show featuring Marie Pantalon, one of her *Mother Lode* characters.

The author welcomes comments and suggestions for subsequent editions of *Women's Voices from the Mother Lode.* Please write c/o Tamarack Books, PO Box 190313, Boise, ID 83719-0313.

Additional copies of *Women's Voices from the Mother Lode* can be found in fine bookstores nationwide or directly from the publisher.

If ordering direct, please include a check for $20.95 (book @ $16.95 plus a shipping/handling charge of $4.00). Idaho residents should send $21.80 (book @ $16.95, shipping/handling $4.00, and Idaho tax $.85).

Send your name, address, and check to:

WVML Orders
Tamarack Books, Inc.
PO Box 190313
Boise, ID 83719-0313

To place orders using MasterCard or Visa,
please call 1–800–962–6657.

If you liked this book, you will enjoy
Women's Voices from the Oregon Trail and
Women's Voices from the Western Frontier
also by Susan G. Butruille.

For information on these or other Tamarack titles
please call 1–800–962–6657.

Ask for our free catalog!